ROLAND BARTHES

A Lover's Discourse

FRAGMENTS

Translated by Richard Howard

PENGUIN BOOKS

PENGUIN BOOKS

Published by the Penguin Group
Penguin Books Ltd, 27 Wrights Lane, London W8 5TZ, England
Penguin Books USA Inc., 375 Hudson Street, New York, New York 10014, USA
Penguin Books Australia Ltd, Ringwood, Victoria, Australia
Penguin Books Canada Ltd, 10 Alcorn Avenue, Toronto, Ontario, Canada M4V 3B2
Penguin Books (NZ) Ltd, 182–190 Wairau Road, Auckland 10, New Zealand

Penguin Books Ltd, Registered Offices: Harmondsworth, Middlesex, England

First published in French as *Fragments d'un discours amoureux*
by Éditions du Seuil 1977
This translation first published in the USA by Farrar,
Straus and Giroux, Inc. 1978
First published in Great Britain by Jonathan Cape Ltd 1979
Published in Penguin Books 1990
5 7 9 10 8 6 4

Printed in England by Clays Ltd, St Ives plc

CONTENTS

A LOVER'S DISCOURSE

The necessity for this book is to be found in the
following consideration: that the lover's discourse
is today *of an extreme solitude*. This discourse is
spoken, perhaps, by thousands of subjects (who
knows?), but warranted by no one; it is completely
forsaken by the surrounding languages: ignored,
disparaged, or derided by them, severed not only
from authority but also from the mechanisms of
authority (sciences, techniques, arts). Once a
discourse is thus driven by its own momentum into
the backwater of the "unreal," exiled from all
gregarity, it has no recourse but to become the
site, however exiguous, of an *affirmation*. That
affirmation is, in short, the subject of the book
which begins here . . .

How this book is constructed

Everything follows from this principle: that the lover is not to be reduced to a simple symptomal subject, but rather that we hear in his voice what is "unreal," i.e., intractable. Whence the choice of a "dramatic" method which renounces examples and rests on the single action of a primary language (no metalanguage). The description of the lover's discourse has been replaced by its simulation, and to that discourse has been restored its fundamental person, the *I*, in order to stage an utterance, not an analysis. What is proposed, then, is a portrait—but not a psychological portrait; instead, a structural one which offers the reader a discursive site: the site of someone speaking within himself, *amorously*, confronting the other (the loved object), who does not speak.

1 Figures

Dis-cursus—originally the action of running here and there, comings and goings, measures taken, "plots and plans": the lover, in fact, cannot keep his mind from racing, taking new measures and plotting against himself. His discourse exists only in outbursts of language, which occur at the whim of trivial, of aleatory circumstances.

These fragments of discourse can be called *figures*. The word is to be understood, not in its rhetorical sense, but rather in its gymnastic or choreographic acceptation; in short, in the Greek meaning: σχῆμα is not the "schema," but, in a much livelier way, the body's gesture caught in action and not contemplated in repose: the body of athletes, orators, statues: what in the straining body can be immobilized. So it is with the lover at grips with his figures: he struggles in a kind of lunatic sport, he spends himself, like an athlete; he "phrases," like an orator; he is caught, stuffed into a role, like a statue. The figure is the lover at work.

Figures take shape insofar as we can recognize, in passing discourse, something that has been read, heard, felt. The figure is outlined (like a sign) and memorable (like an image or a tale). A figure is established if at least someone can say: *"That's so true! I recognize that scene of language."* For certain operations of their art, linguists make use of a vague entity which they call linguistic feeling; in order to constitute figures, we require neither more nor less than this guide: amorous feeling.

Ultimately it is unimportant whether the text's dispersion is rich here and poor there; there are nodes, blanks, many figures break off short; some, being hypostases of the whole of the lover's discourse, have just the rarity—the poverty—of essences: What is to be said of Languor, of the Image, of the Love Letter, since it is the whole of the lover's discourse which is woven of languorous desire, of the image-repertoire, of declarations? But he who utters this discourse and shapes its episodes does not know that a book is to be made of them; he does not yet know that as a good cultural subject he should neither repeat nor contradict himself, nor take the whole for the part; all he knows is that what passes through his mind at a certain moment is *marked,* like the printout of a code (in other times, this would have been the code of courtly love, or the Carte du Tendre).

Each of us can fill in this code according to his own history; rich or poor, the figure must be there, the site (the compartment) must be reserved for it. It is as if there were an amorous Topic, whose figure was a site (topos). Now the property of a Topic is to be somewhat empty: a Topic is statutorily half coded, half projective (or projective because coded). What we have been able to say below about waiting, anxiety, memory is no more than a modest supplement offered to the reader to be made free with, to be added to, subtracted from, and passed on to others: around the figure, the players pass the handkerchief which sometimes, by a final parenthesis, is held a second longer before handing it on. (Ideally, the book would be a cooperative: "To the United Readers and Lovers.")

What reads as the heading of each figure is not its definition but its argument. *Argumentum:* "exposition, account, summary, plot outline, invented narrative"; I should add: instrument of distancing, signboard à la Brecht. This argument does not refer to the amorous subject and what he is (no one external to this subject, no discourse on love), but to what he says. If there is such a figure as "Anxiety," it is because the subject sometimes exclaims (without any concern for the clinical sense of the word): "I am having an anxiety attack!" Anxiety, Anguish . . . *"Angoscia!"* Callas sings somewhere. The figure is a kind of opera aria; just as this aria is identified, memorized, and manipulated through its *incipit* ("When I am laid," *"Pleurez, mes yeux," "Lucevan le stelle," "Piangerò la mia sorte"*), so the figure takes its departure from a turn of phrase, a kind of verse, refrain, or cantillation which articulates it in the darkness.

It is said that words alone have specific uses, not sentences; but underneath each figure lies a sentence, frequently an unknown (unconscious?) one, which has its use in the signifying economy of the amorous subject. This matrix-sentence (here merely postulated) is not a "saturated" one, not a completed message. Its active principle is not what it says but what it articulates: by and large, it is only a "syntactical aria," a "mode of construction." For instance, if the subject awaits the loved object at a rendezvous, a sentence-aria keeps running through his head: *"All the same, it's not fair . . .";* *"he/she could have . . .";* *"he/she knows perfectly well . . .":* knows what? It doesn't matter, the figure "Waiting" is already formed. Such sentences are matrices of figures precisely because they remain suspended: they utter the affect, then break off, their role is filled. The words are never crazed (at most perverse), but the syntax is: is it not on the level of the sentence that the subject seeks his place—and fails to find it—or finds a false place imposed upon him by language? Underneath the figure, there is something of the "verbal hallucination" (Freud, Lacan): a mutilated sentence which is generally limited to its syntactical portion (*"Even though you are . . ."* *"If you were still . . ."*). Whence the emotion of every figure: even the mildest bears within it the terror of a *suspense:* in it, I hear the tempestuous, Neptunian *quos ego . . .*

2 Order

Throughout any love life, figures occur to the lover without any order, for on each occasion they depend on an (internal or external) accident. Confronting each of these incidents (what "befalls" him), the amorous subject draws on the reservoir (the thesaurus?) of figures, depending on the needs, the injunctions, or the pleasures of his image-repertoire. Each figure explodes, vibrates in and of itself like a sound severed from any tune—or is repeated to satiety, like the motif of a hovering music. No logic links the figures, determines their contiguity: the figures are non-syntagmatic, non-narrative; they are Erinyes; they stir, collide, subside, return, vanish with no more order than the flight of mosquitoes. Amorous *dis-cursus* is not dialectical; it turns like a perpetual calendar, an encyclopedia of affective culture (there is something of Bouvard and Pécuchet in the lover).

In linguistic terms, one might say that the figures are distributional but not integrative; they always remain on the same level: the lover speaks in bundles of sentences but does not integrate these sentences on a higher level, into a work; his is a horizontal discourse: no transcendence, no deliverance, no novel (though a great deal of the fictive). Every amorous episode can be, of course, endowed with a meaning: it is generated, develops, and dies; it follows a path which it is always possible to interpret according to a causality or a finality—even, if need be, which can be moralized (*"I was out of my mind, I'm over it now" "Love is a trap which must be avoided from now on"* etc.): this is the *love story,* subjugated to the great narrative Other, to that general opinion which disparages any excessive force and wants the subject himself to reduce the great imaginary current, the orderless, endless stream which is passing through him, to a painful, morbid crisis of which he must be cured, which he must "get over" ("It develops, grows, causes suffering, and passes away" in the fashion of some Hippocratic disease): the love story (the "episode," the "adventure") is the tribute the lover must pay to the world in order to be reconciled with it.

Very different is the discourse, the soliloquy, the *aside* which accompanies this story (and this history), *without ever knowing it*. It is the very principle of this discourse (and of the text which represents it) that its figures cannot be *classified:* organized, hierarchized, arranged with a view to an end (a settlement): there are no first figures, no last figures. To let it be understood that there was no question here of a love story (or of the history of a love), to discourage the temptation of meaning, it was necessary to choose an *absolutely insignificant* order. Hence we have subjugated the series of figures (inevitable as any series is, since the book is by its status obliged to *progress*) to a pair of arbitrary factors: that of nomination and that of the alphabet. Each of these arbitrary factors is nonetheless tempered: one by semantic necessity (among all the nouns in the dictionary, a figure can receive only two or three), the other by the age-old convention which decides the order of our alphabet. Hence we have avoided the wiles of pure chance, which might indeed have produced logical sequences; for we must not, one mathematician tells us, "underestimate the power of chance to engender monsters"; the monster, in this case, would have been, emerging from a certain order of the figures, a "philosophy of love" where we must look for no more than its affirmation.

3 References

In order to compose this amorous subject, pieces of various origin have been "put together." Some come from an ordinary reading, that of Goethe's *Werther.* Some come from insistent readings (Plato's *Symposium,* Zen, psychoanalysis, certain Mystics, Nietzsche, German lieder). Some come from occasional readings. Some come from conversations with friends. And there are some which come from my own life.

What comes from books and from friends occasionally appears in the margin of the text, in the form of names (for the books) and initials (for the friends). The refer-

ences supplied in this fashion are not authoritative but
amical: I am not invoking guarantees, merely recalling, by
a kind of salute given in passing, what has seduced, con-
vinced, or what has momentarily given the delight of understanding (of being understood?). Therefore, these
reminders of reading, of listening, have been left in the
frequently uncertain, incompleted state suitable to a discourse whose occasion is indeed the memory of the sites
(books, encounters) where such and such a thing has been
read, spoken, heard. For if the author here lends his "culture" to the amorous subject, in exchange the amorous
subject affords him the innocence of his image-repertoire,
indifferent to the proprieties of knowledge.

So it is a lover who speaks and who says:

"I am engulfed,
I succumb . . ."

s'abîmer / to be engulfed
Outburst of annihilation which affects the amorous
subject in despair or fulfillment.

Werther

1.   Either woe or well-being, sometimes I have a crav-
ing *to be engulfed*. This morning (in the country), the
weather is mild, overcast. I am suffering (from some incident). The notion of suicide occurs to me, pure of any
resentment (not blackmailing anyone); an insipid notion;
it alters nothing ("breaks" nothing), matches the color
(the silence, the desolation) of this morning.

Another day, in the rain, we're waiting for the boat at the
lake; from happiness, this time, the same outburst of
annihilation sweeps through me. This is how it happens
sometimes, misery or joy engulfs me, without any particular tumult ensuing: nor any pathos: I am dissolved, not
dismembered; I fall, I flow, I melt. Such thoughts—
grazed, touched, tested (the way you test the water with
your foot)—can recur. Nothing solemn about them.
This is exactly what *gentleness* is.

2.   The crisis of engulfment can come from a wound,

WERTHER: "In such thoughts I am engulfed, I succumb, under the power
of these magnificent visions . . . I shall see her . . . Everything, yes,
everything, as though engulfed by an abyss, vanishes into this prospect."

Tristan
Baudelaire
but also from a fusion: we die together from loving each other: an open death, by dilution into the ether, a closed death of the shared grave.

Engulfment is a moment of hypnosis. A suggestion functions, which commands me to swoon without killing myself. Whence, perhaps, the gentleness of the abyss: I have no responsibility here, the act (of dying) is not up to me: I entrust myself, I transmit myself (to whom? to God, to Nature, to everything, except to the other).

Ruysbroeck

3.   Therefore, on those occasions when I am engulfed, it is because there is no longer any place for me anywhere, not even in death. The image of the other—to which I was glued, on which I lived—no longer exists; sometimes this is a (futile) catastrophe which seems to remove the image forever, sometimes it is an excessive happiness which enables me to unite with the image; in any case, severed or united, dissolved or discrete, I am nowhere *gathered together;* opposite, neither you nor me, nor death, nor anything else *to talk to.*

(Strangely, it is in the extreme action of the amorous Image-repertoire—annihilation as a consequence of driving out the image or of being identified with it—that there occurs a fall of this Image-repertoire: for the brief interval of a vacillation, I lose my structure as a lover: this is a factitious mourning, without work to do: something like a non-site.)

4.   In love with death? An exaggeration to say, with

TRISTAN: "In the blessed abyss of the infinite ether, in your sublime soul, boundless immensity, I sink and am engulfed, unconscious, O bliss!" (Isolde's death).

BAUDELAIRE: "Some pink and blue evening, we shall exchange a single impulse, a kind of long sob, heavy with farewells" (*"La Mort des amants"*).

RUYSBROECK: ". . . The repose of the abyss."

Keats, *half in love with easeful death:* death liberated
from dying. Then I have this fantasy: a gentle hemorrhage
which flows from no specific point in my body, an *almost*
immediate consumption, calculated so that I might have
the time to abate my suffering without yet having died.
Fleetingly I establish myself within a false conception of
death (false the way a key is "falsified" by warping): I
conceive of death *beside me:* I conceive of it according to
an unthought logic, I drift outside of the fatal couple
which links life and death by opposing them to each other.

5.   Is the abyss no more than an expedient annihilation? It would not be difficult for me to read the abyss,
not as a repose, but as an *emotion.* I mask my mourning
by an evasion; I dilute myself, I swoon in order to escape
that density, that clogging which makes me into a *responsible* subject: I come out: it is ecstasy.

Sartre

Rue du Cherche-Midi, after a difficult evening, X was
explaining very carefully, his voice exact, his sentences
well-formed, far from anything inexpressible, that sometimes he longed to swoon; he regretted never being able to
disappear at will.
His words were saying that he meant then to succumb to
his weakness, not to resist the wounds the world inflicted
upon him; but at the same time he was substituting for this
failing strength another strength, another affirmation: *I
assume toward and against everything a denial of courage,
hence a denial of morality:* that is what X's voice was
saying.

SARTRE: On swooning and anger as evasions, *The Emotions.*

The Absent One

absence / absence

Any episode of language which stages the absence
of the loved object—whatever its cause and its
duration—and which tends to transform this
absence into an ordeal of abandonment.

1.   Many lieder, songs, and *mélodies* about the beloved's absence. And yet this classic figure is not to be
Werther   found in Werther. The reason is simple: here the loved
object (Charlotte) does not move; it is the amorous subject (Werther) who, at a certain moment, departs. Now,
absence can exist only as a consequence of the other: it is
the other who leaves, it is I who remain. The other is in a
condition of perpetual departure, of journeying; the other
is, by vocation, migrant, fugitive; I—I who love, by converse vocation, am sedentary, motionless, at hand, in expectation, nailed to the spot, *in suspense*—like a package
in some forgotten corner of a railway station. Amorous
absence functions in a single direction, expressed by the
one who stays, never by the one who leaves: an always
present *I* is constituted only by confrontation with an always absent *you*. To speak this absence is from the start
to propose that the subject's place and the other's place
cannot permute; it is to say: "I am loved less than I
love."

2.   Historically, the discourse of absence is carried on
by the Woman: Woman is sedentary, Man hunts, jour-

Hugo

neys; Woman is faithful (she waits), man is fickle (he sails away, he cruises). It is Woman who gives shape to absence, elaborates its fiction, for she has time to do so; she weaves and she sings; the Spinning Songs express both immobility (by the hum of the Wheel) and absence (far away, rhythms of travel, sea surges, cavalcades). It follows that in any man who utters the other's absence *something feminine* is declared: this man who waits and who suffers from his waiting is miraculously feminized. A man is not feminized because he is inverted but because he is in love. (Myth and utopia: the origins have belonged, the future will belong to the subjects *in whom there is something feminine.*)

E.B.

3.　　Sometimes I have no difficulty enduring absence. Then I am "normal": I fall in with the way "everyone" endures the departure of a "beloved person"; I diligently obey the training by which I was very early accustomed to be separated from my mother—which nonetheless remained, at its source, a matter of suffering (not to say hysteria). I behave as a well-weaned subject; I can feed myself, *meanwhile,* on other things besides the maternal breast.

This endured absence is nothing more or less than forgetfulness. I am, intermittently, unfaithful. This is the condition of my survival; for if I did not forget, I should die. The lover who doesn't forget *sometimes* dies of excess, exhaustion, and tension of memory (like Werther).

Werther

(As a child, I didn't forget: interminable days, abandoned days, when the Mother was working far away; I would go,

HUGO: "Woman, whom do you weep for?" "The absent one" (*"L'Absent,"* a poem set to music by Fauré).
E.R.· Letter.

evenings, to wait for her at the U^bis bus stop, Sèvres-Babylone; the buses would pass one after the other, she wasn't in any of them.)

4.   I waken out of this forgetfulness very quickly. In great haste, I reconstitute a memory, a confusion. A (classic) word comes from the body, which expresses the emotion of absence: *to sigh:* "to sigh for the bodily presence": the two halves of the androgyne sigh for each other, as if each breath, being incomplete, sought to mingle with the other: the image of the embrace, in that it melts the two images into a single one: in amorous absence, I am, sadly, an *unglued image* that dries, yellows, shrivels.

Ruysbroeck
Symposium
Diderot

(But isn't desire always the same, whether the object is present or absent? Isn't the object *always* absent? —This isn't the same languor: there are two words: *Pothos,* desire for the absent being, and *Himéros,* the more burning desire for the present being.)

Greek

5.   Endlessly I sustain the discourse of the beloved's absence; actually a preposterous situation; the other is absent as referent, present as allocutory. This singular distortion generates a kind of insupportable present; I am wedged between two tenses, that of the reference and that of the allocution: you have gone (which I lament), you are here (since I am addressing you). Whereupon I know what the present, that difficult tense, is: a pure portion of anxiety.

DIDEROT: "Bring your lips to mine/so that out of my mouth/my soul may pass into yours" (*Chanson dans le goût de la romance*).

Absence persists—I must endure it. Hence I will *manipulate* it: transform the distortion of time into oscillation, produce rhythm, make an entrance onto the stage of language (language is born of absence: the child has made himself a doll out of a spool, throws it away and picks it up again, miming the mother's departure and return: a paradigm is created). Absence becomes an active practice, a *business* (which keeps me from doing anything else); there is a creation of a fiction which has many roles (doubts, reproaches, desires, melancholies). This staging
of language postpones the other's death: a very short interval, we are told, separates the time during which the child still believes his mother to be absent and the time during which he believes her to be already dead. To manipulate absence is to extend this interval, to delay as long as possible the moment when the other might topple sharply from absence into death.

Winnicott

6.   Frustration would have Presence as its figure (I see the other every day, yet I am not satisfied thereby: the object is actually there yet continues, in terms of my image-repertoire, to be absent for me). Whereas castration has Intermittence as its figure (I agree to leave the other for a while, "without tears," I assume the grief of the relation, I am able to *forget*). Absence is the figure of privation; simultaneously, I desire and I need. Desire is squashed against need: that is the obsessive phenomenon of all amorous sentiment.

Ruysbroeck

("Desire is present, ardent, eternal: but God is higher still, and the raised arms of Desire never attain to the adored plenitude." The discourse of Absence is a text with two ideograms: there are *the raised arms of Desire,* and there are *the wide-open arms of Need*. I oscillate, I vacillate between the phallic image of the raised arms, and the babyish image of the wide-open arms.)

7.   I take a seat, alone, in a café; people come over and speak to me; I feel that I am sought after, surrounded, flattered. But the other is absent; I invoke the other inwardly to keep me on the brink of this mundane complacency, a temptation. I appeal to the other's "truth" (the truth of which the other gives me the sensation) against the hysteria of seduction into which I feel myself slipping. I make the other's absence responsible for my worldliness: *I invoke* the other's protection, the other's return: let the other appear, take me away, like a mother who comes looking for her child, from this worldly brilliance, from this social infatuation, let the other restore to me "the religious intimacy, the gravity" of the lover's world. (X once told me that love had protected him against worldliness: coteries, ambitions, advancements, interferences, alliances, secessions, roles, powers: love had made him into a social catastrophe, to his delight.)

8.   A Buddhist Koan says: "The master holds the disciple's head underwater for a long, long time; gradually the bubbles become fewer; at the last moment, the master pulls the disciple out and revives him: when you have craved truth as you crave air, then you will know what truth is."
The absence of the other holds my head underwater; gradually I drown, my air supply gives out: it is by this asphyxia that I reconstitute my "truth" and that I prepare what in love is Intractable.

s.s.: Koan reported by S.S.

s.s.

"Adorable!"

adorable / adorable

Not managing to name the specialty of his desire
for the loved being, the amorous subject falls back
on this rather stupid word: *adorable!*

1. "One lovely September day, I went out to do some
errands. Paris was *adorable* that morning . . . ," etc.
A host of perceptions suddenly come together to form a
dazzling impression (to dazzle is ultimately to prevent
sight, to prevent speech): the weather, the season, the
light, the boulevard, the Parisians out walking, shopping,
all held within what *already* has its vocation as memory: a

Diderot   scene, in short, the hieroglyph of kindliness (as Greuze
might have painted it), the good humor of desire. All
Paris is within my grasp, without my wanting to grasp it:
neither languor nor lust. I forget all the reality in Paris
which exceeds its charm: history, labor, money, merchandise—all the harshness of big cities; here I see only
the object of an aesthetically *restrained* desire. From the
top of Père Lachaise, Rastignac hurled his challenge to the

Balzac   city: *Between the two of us now;* I say to Paris: *Adorable!*

After an impression of the night before, I wake up soft-
ened by a happy thought: "X was adorable last night."
This is the memory of . . . what? Of what the Greeks

Greek   called *charis:* "the sparkle of the eyes, the body's luminous
beauty, the radiance of the desirable being"; and I may

DIDEROT, like Lessing, elaborates a theory of the *pregnant moment.*

even add, just as in the ancient *charis,* the notion—the hope—that the loved object will bestow itself upon my desire.

2.   By a singular logic, the amorous subject perceives the other as a Whole (in the fashion of Paris on an autumn afternoon), and, at the same time, this Whole seems to him to involve a remainder, which he cannot express. It is the other *as a whole* who produces in him an aesthetic vision: he praises the other for being perfect, he glorifies himself for having chosen this perfect other; he imagines that the other wants to be loved, as he himself would want to be loved, not for one or another of his qualities, but for *everything,* and this *everything* he bestows upon the other in the form of a blank word, for the Whole cannot be inventoried without being diminished: in *Adorable!* there is no residual quality, but only the *everything* of affect. Yet, at the same time that *adorable* says everything, it also says what is lacking in everything; it seeks to designate that site of the other to which my desire clings *in a special way,* but this site cannot be designated; about it I shall never know anything; my language will always fumble, stammer in order to attempt to express it, but I can never produce anything but a blank word, an empty vocable, which is the zero degree of all the sites where my very special desire for this particular other (and for no other) will form.

3.   I encounter millions of bodies in my life; of these millions, I may desire some hundreds; but of these hundreds, I love only one. The other with whom I am in love designates for me the specialty of my desire.

Lacan

Proust

This choice, so rigorous that it retains only the Unique, constitutes, it is said, the difference between the analytical transference and the amorous transference; one is universal, the other specific. It has taken many accidents, many surprising coincidences (and perhaps many efforts), for me to find the Image which, out of a thousand, suits my desire. Herein a great enigma, to which I shall never possess the key: Why is it that I desire So-and-so? Why is it that I desire So-and-so lastingly, longingly? Is it the whole of So-and-so I desire (a silhouette, a shape, a mood)? And, in that case, what is it in this loved body which has the vocation of a fetish for me? What perhaps incredibly tenuous portion—what accident? The way a nail is cut, a tooth broken slightly aslant, a lock of hair, a way of spreading the fingers while talking, while smoking? About all these *folds* of the body, I want to say that they are *adorable*. *Adorable* means: this is my desire, insofar as it is unique: "That's it! That's it exactly (which I love)!" Yet the more I experience the specialty of my desire, the less I can give it a name; to the precision of the target corresponds a wavering of the name; what is characteristic of desire, proper to desire, can produce only an impropriety of the utterance. Of this failure of language, there remains only one trace: the word "adorable" (the right translation of "adorable" would be the Latin *ipse:* it is the self, himself, herself, in person).

4.   *Adorable* is the futile vestige of a fatigue—the fatigue of language itself. From word to word, I struggle to put "into other words" the ipseity of my Image, to

LACAN: "It is not every day that you encounter what is so constituted as to give you precisely the image of your desire."
PROUST: Scene of the specialty of desire: Jupien and Charlus meet in the courtyard of the Hôtel de Guermantes (at the beginning of *Cities of the Plain*).

express improperly the propriety of my desire: a journey at whose end my final philosophy can only be to recognize —and to practice—tautology. *The adorable is what is adorable.* Or again: I adore you because you are adorable, I love you because I love you. What thereby closes off the lover's language is the very thing which has instituted it: fascination. For to describe fascination can never, *in the last analysis,* exceed this utterance: "I am fascinated." Having attained the end of language, where it can merely repeat *its last word* like a scratched record, I intoxicate myself upon its affirmation: is not tautology that preposterous state in which are to be found, all values being confounded, the glorious end of the logical operation, the obscenity of stupidity, and the explosion of the Nietzschean *yes?*

Nietzsche

The Intractable

affirmation / affirmation

Against and in spite of everything, the subject
affirms love as *value*.

1.   Despite the difficulties of my story, despite dis-
comforts, doubts, despairs, despite impulses to be done
with it, I unceasingly affirm love, within myself, as a
value. Though I listen to all the arguments which the most
divergent systems employ to demystify, to limit, to erase,
in short to depreciate love, I persist: "I know, I know, but
all the same . . ." I refer the devaluations of love to a
kind of obscurantist ethic, to a let's-pretend realism,
against which I erect the realism of value: I counter
whatever "doesn't work" in love with the affirmation of
what is worthwhile. This stubbornness is love's protest:
for all the wealth of "good reasons" for loving differently,
loving better, loving without being in love, etc., a stubborn
voice is raised which lasts *a little longer:* the voice of the
Intractable lover.

The world subjects every enterprise to an alternative; that
of success or failure, of victory or defeat. I protest by
another logic: I am simultaneously and contradictorily
happy and wretched; "to succeed" or "to fail" have for
me only contingent, provisional meanings (which doesn't
keep my sufferings and my desires from being violent);
what inspires me, secretly and stubbornly, is not a tactic: I

Pelléas

PELLÉAS: "What's the matter? You don't seem to be happy." "Oh yes,
I am happy, but I am sad."

accept and I affirm, beyond truth and falsehood, beyond success and failure; I have withdrawn from all finality, I live according to chance (as is evidenced by the fact that the figures of my discourse occur to me like so many dice casts). Flouted in my enterprise (as it happens), I emerge from it neither victor nor vanquished: I am tragic.

(Someone tells me: this kind of love is not viable. But how can you *evaluate* viability? Why is the viable a Good Thing? Why is it better to *last* than to *burn?*)

Schelling

2. This morning, I must get off an "important" letter right away—one on which the success of a certain undertaking depends; but instead I write a love letter—which I do not send. I gladly abandon dreary tasks, rational scruples, reactive undertakings imposed by the world, for the sake of a useless task deriving from a dazzling Duty: the lover's Duty. I perform, discreetly, lunatic chores; I am the sole witness of my lunacy. What love lays bare in me is *energy*. Everything I do has a meaning (hence I can *live,* without whining), but this meaning is an ineffable finality: it is merely the meaning of my strength. The painful, guilty, melancholy inflections, the whole reactive side of my everyday life is reversed. Werther praises his own tension, which he affirms, in contrast to Albert's platitudes. Born of literature, able to speak only with the help of its worn codes, yet I am alone with my strength, doomed *to my own philosophy*.

Werther

3. In the Christian West, until today, all strength passes through the Interpreter, as a type (in Nietzschean

SCHELLING: "The essence of tragedy is . . . a real conflict between the subject's freedom and an objective necessity, a conflict which is ended not by the defeat of one or the other but because both, at once victors and vanquished, appear in a perfect indifferentiation."

WERTHER: "Oh, my dear friend, if to tender one's whole being is to give evidence of strength, why should an excessive tension be weakness?"

J.-L.B.

terms, the Judaic High Priest). But the strength of love cannot be shifted, be put into the hands of an Interpreter; it remains here, on the level of language, enchanted, intractable. Here the type is not the Priest, it is the Lover.

4.   Love has two affirmations. First of all, when the lover encounters the other, there is an immediate affirmation (psychologically: dazzlement, enthusiasm, exaltation, mad projection of a fulfilled future: I am devoured by desire, the impulse to be happy): I say *yes* to everything (blinding myself). There follows a long tunnel: my first *yes* is riddled by doubts, love's *value* is ceaselessly threatened by depreciation: this is the moment of melancholy passion, the rising of resentment and of oblation. Yet I

Nietzsche

can emerge from this tunnel; I can "surmount," without liquidating; what I have affirmed a first time, I can once again affirm, without repeating it, for then what I affirm is the affirmation, not its contingency: I affirm the first encounter in its difference, I desire its return, not its repetition. I say to the other (old or new): *Let us begin again.*

J.-L.B.: Conversation.
NIETZSCHE: All this comes from Deleuze's account of the affirmation of the affirmation.

The Tip of the Nose

altération / alteration

Abrupt production, within the amorous field, of a
counter-image of the loved object. According to
minor incidents or tenuous features, the subject
suddenly sees the good Image alter and capsize.

Ruysbroeck
Dostoevsky

1.   Ruysbroeck has been buried for five years; he is
exhumed; his body is intact and pure (of course—otherwise, there would be no story); *but* "there was only the tip
of the nose which bore a faint but certain trace of corruption." In the other's perfect and "embalmed" figure (for
that is the degree to which it fascinates me) I perceive
suddenly a speck of corruption. This speck is a tiny one: a
gesture, a word, an object, a garment, something unex-
pected which appears (which dawns) from a region I had
never even suspected, and suddenly attaches the loved object to a *commonplace* world. Could the other be vulgar,
whose elegance and originality I had so religiously
hymned? Here is a gesture by which is revealed a being of
another race. I am *flabbergasted:* I hear a counter-rhythm:
something like a syncope in the lovely phrase of the loved
being, the noise of a rip in the smooth envelope of the
Image.
(Like the Jesuit Kircher's hen, released from hypnosis by
a light tap, I am temporarily de-fascinated, not without
pain.)

DOSTOEVSKY: The death of Father Zossima: the noxious smell of the
corpse (*The Brothers Karamazov*).

2.   It is as if the alteration of the Image occurs when *I*

Symposium

am ashamed for the other (the fear of this shame, according to Phaedrus, kept the Greek lovers in the ways of the
Good, each obliged to care for his own image in the
other's eyes). Now, shame comes from subjection: the
other, because of a trivial incident which only my per-
spicacity or my madness apprehend, suddenly appears—is
revealed, is exposed, in the photographic sense of the
term—as *subjected* to an instance which is itself of a
servile order: I suddenly see the other (a question of
vision) busily or frenziedly or just insistently abiding by,
respecting, yielding to worldly rites by which some sort of
recognition is hoped for. For the bad Image is not a
wicked image; it is a *paltry* image: it shows me the other
caught up in the platitude of the social world—commonplace. (Or again: the other alters if he or she sides with

Heine

the banalities the world professes in order to depreciate
love: the other becomes gregarious.)

3.   Once, speaking to me of ourselves, the other said:
"a relation of quality"; this phrase was repugnant to me:
it came suddenly from outside, flattening the specialty of
the rapport by a conformist formula.

Quite frequently, it is by language that the other is altered;
the other speaks a different word, and I hear rumbling
menacingly *a whole other world,* which is the world of the
other. When Albertine drops the trivial phrase "get her

Proust

pot broken," the Proustian narrator is horrified, for it is
the dreaded ghetto of female homosexuality, of crude
cruising, which is suddenly revealed thereby: a whole

HEINE: *"Sie sassen und tranken am Teetisch . . ."* (*"Lyrisches Intermezzo"*).
PROUST: *The Captive.*

scene through the keyhole of language. The word is of a tenuous chemical substance which performs the most violent alterations: the other, long maintained in the cocoon of my own discourse, suggests, by a word escaping unchecked from his or her lips, the languages which can be *borrowed,* and which consequently others have lent.

4.   Sometimes, too, the other appears to me as subjected to a desire. But what then constitutes the corruption is not in my eyes a desire which is formed, named, proposed, aimed—in which case I would be, more simply, jealous (which derives from another tonality); it is only a nascent desire, a whiff of desire which I detect in the other, without the other's being really conscious of it: I see the other, in conversation, stir, multiply, *perform to excess,* assume a position of demand with regard to a third party, as though hung upon that third party in order to seduce him. Observe any such encounter carefully: you will see this subject (discreetly, mundanely) infatuated by this other, driven to establish with this other a warmer, more demanding, more flattering relation: I surprise the other, so to speak, in the act of self-inflation. I perceive *an infatuation of being,* which is not so far from what Sade would have called *an effervescence of countenance* ("I saw the sperm shooting from his eyes"); and, should the solicited partner respond in the same manner, the scene becomes ridiculous: I have the vision of two peacocks spreading their tails, each in front of the other. The image

Flaubert

FLAUBERT: "A sudden gust of wind lifted the cloths, and they saw two peacocks, a male and a female. The female crouched motionless, legs bent, rump in the air. The male strutted around her, fanning out his tail, puffing his feathers, clucking, then leaped upon her, spreading his wings until he covered her like a cradle, and the two huge birds swayed together . . ." (*Bouvard et Pécuchet*).

is corrupted, because the person I suddenly see is then *another* (and no longer the other), a stranger (and mad?).

Gide

(For example, in the train from Biskra, Gide, in complicity with the three Algerian schoolboys, "gasping, panting" before his wife, who was pretending to read, looked like "a criminal or a madman." Is not any other desire but mine *insane?*)

UNORTHODOX

5.   The lover's discourse is usually a smooth envelope which encases the Image, a very gentle glove around the loved being. It is a devout, orthodox discourse. When the Image alters, the envelope of devotion rips apart; a shock capsizes my own language. Wounded by a remark he overhears, Werther suddenly sees Charlotte in the guise of a gossip, he includes her within the group of her companions with whom she is chattering (she is no longer the other, but one among others), and then says disdainfully: "my good little women" (*meine Weibchen*). A *blasphemy* abruptly rises to the subject's lips and disrespectfully explodes the lover's benediction; he is possessed by a demon who speaks through his mouth, out of which emerge, as in the fairy tales, no longer flowers, but toads. Horrible ebb of the Image. (The horror of spoiling is even stronger than the anxiety of losing.)

Werther

GIDE: *Et nunc manet in te.*

Agony

angoisse / anxiety

The amorous subject, according to one
contingency or another, feels swept away by the
fear of a danger, an injury, an abandonment, a
revulsion—a sentiment he expresses under the
name of *anxiety*.

1.   Tonight I came back to the hotel alone; the other
has decided to return later on. The anxieties are already
here, like the poison already prepared (jealousy, abandonment, restlessness); they merely wait for a little time
to pass in order to be able to declare themselves with some
propriety. I pick up a book and take a sleeping pill,
"calmly." The silence of this huge hotel is echoing, indifferent, idiotic (faint murmur of draining bathtubs); the
furniture and the lamps are stupid; nothing *friendly* that
might warm ("I'm cold, let's go back to Paris"). Anxiety
mounts; I observe its progress, like Socrates chatting (as I
am reading) and feeling the cold of the hemlock rising in
his body; I *hear it* identify itself moving up, like an inexorable figure, against the background of *the things that
are here*.

(And if, *so that something might happen,* I were to make
a vow?)

2.   The psychotic lives in the terror of breakdown
(against which the various psychoses are merely de-
fenses). But "the clinical fear of breakdown is the fear of

Winnicott

a breakdown which has already been experienced (*primi-tive agony*) . . . and there are moments when a patient needs to be told that the breakdown, fear of which is wrecking his life, has already occurred." Similarly, it seems, for the lover's anxiety: it is the fear of a mourning which has already occurred, at the very origin of love, from the moment when I was first "ravished." Someone would have to be able to tell me: "Don't be anxious any more—you've already lost him/her."

To Love Love

annulation / annulment

Explosion of language during which the subject
manages to annul the loved object under the
volume of love itself: by a specifically amorous
perversion, it is love the subject loves, not the
object.

Werther

1.   Charlotte is quite insipid; she is the paltry character of a powerful, tormented, flamboyant drama staged
by the subject Werther; by a kindly decision of this subject, a colorless object is placed in the center of the stage
and there adored, idolized, *taken to task,* covered with
discourse, with prayers (and perhaps, surreptitiously, with
invectives); as if she were a huge motionless hen huddled
amid her feathers, around which circles a slightly mad
cock.

Enough that, in a flash, I should see the other in the guise
of an inert object, like a kind of stuffed doll, for me to
shift my desire from this annulled object to my desire
itself; it is my desire I desire, and the loved being is no
more than its tool. I rejoice at the thought of such a great
cause, which leaves far behind it the person whom I have
made into its pretext (at least this is what I tell myself,
happy to raise myself by lowering the other): I sacrifice
the image to the Image-repertoire. And if a day comes
when I must bring myself to renounce the other, the violent mourning which then grips me is the mourning of the
Image-repertoire itself: it was a beloved structure, and I
weep for the loss of love, not of him or her. (I want to go

Gide

back there, like the imprisoned child of Poitiers who
wanted to get back to her big cave Malempia.)

2. ⎪ Here then the other is annulled by love: I derive a
certain advantage from this annulment; should an acci-
dental injury threaten me (a notion of jealousy, for example), I reabsorb it into the magnificence and the abstraction of amorous sentiment: I soothe myself by desiring what, being absent, can no longer harm me. Yet,
immediately thereafter, I suffer at seeing the other (whom
I love) thus diminished, reduced, and somehow excluded
from the sentiment which he or she has provoked. I feel
myself to be guilty and I blame myself for abandoning the
other. A turnabout occurs: I seek to disannul it, I force
myself to suffer once again.

cortezia

To Be Ascetic

askesis

Whether he feels guilty with regard to the loved
being, or whether he seeks to impress that being
by representing his unhappiness, the amorous
subject outlines an ascetic behavior of
self-punishment (in life style, dress, etc.).

1.   Since I am guilty of this, of that (I have—I assign
myself—a thousand reasons for being so), I shall punish
myself, I shall chasten by body: cut my hair very short,
conceal my eyes behind dark glasses (a way of taking the
veil), devote myself to the study of some serious and abstract branch of learning. I shall get up early and work
while it is still dark outside, like a monk. I shall be very
patient, a little sad, in a word, *worthy,* as suits a man of
resentment. I shall (hysterically) signify my mourning
(the mourning which I assign myself) in my dress, my
haircut, the regularity of my habits. This will be a gentle
retreat; just that slight degree of retreat necessary to the
proper functioning of a discrete pathos.

2.   Askesis (the impulse toward askesis) is addressed
to the other: turn back, look at me, see what you have
made of me. It is a blackmail: I raise before the other the
figure of my own disappearance, as it will surely occur, if
the other does not yield (to what?).

Atopos

atopos / atopos

The loved being is recognized by the amorous
subject as "atopos" (a qualification given to
Socrates by his interlocutors), i.e., unclassifiable,
of a ceaselessly unforeseen originality.

Nietzsche

1.   The *atopia* of Socrates is linked to Eros (Socrates
is courted by Alcibiades) and to the numbfish (Socrates
electrifies and benumbs Meno). The other whom I love
and who fascinates me is *atopos*. I cannot classify the
other, for the other is, precisely, Unique, the singular
Image which has miraculously come to correspond to the
specialty of my desire. The other is the figure of my truth,
and cannot be imprisoned in any stereotype (which is the
truth of others).

Yet I have loved or will love several times in my life. Does
this mean, then, that my desire, quite special as it may be,
is linked to a type? Does this mean that my desire is
classifiable? Is there, among all the beings I have loved, a
common characteristic, just one, however tenuous (a
nose, a skin, a look), which allows me to say: that's my
type! "Just my type" or "not my type at all"—cruising
slogans: then is the lover merely a choosier cruiser, who
spends his life looking for "his type"? In which corner of
the adverse body must I read my truth?

NIETZSCHE: On the *atopia* of Socrates, Michel Guerin's *Nietzsche,
Socrate héroïque.*

2.　　I surprise the other's *atopia* on his/her face each time I read there a certain tremendous innocence: the other knows nothing of the harm he or she has done me—or, to put it less rhetorically, of the harm he or she has given me. Is not the innocent party unclassifiable (hence suspect in every society, which "knows where it is" only where it can classify Faults)?

X had many "character traits" by which it was not difficult to classify him (he was "indiscreet," "wily," "indolent," etc.), but I had had, two or three times, occasion to read in his eyes an expression of such an *innocence* (no other word) that I persisted, whatever happened, in setting him, so to speak, aside from himself, outside of his own character. At that moment, I was exonerating him from all criticism or commentary. As innocence, *atopia* resists description, definition, language, which is *maya,* classification of Names (of Faults). Being Atopic, the other makes language indecisive: one cannot speak *of* the other, *about* the other; every attribute is false, painful, erroneous, awkward: the other is *unqualifiable* (this would be the true meaning of *atopos*).

3.　　Confronted with the other's brilliant originality, I never feel myself to be *atopos,* but rather classified (like an all-too-familiar dossier). Sometimes, though, I manage to suspend the action of the unequal images ("If only I could be as original, as strong as the other!"); I divine that the true site of originality and strength is neither the other nor myself, but our relation itself. It is the originality of the relation which must be conquered. Most of my injuries come from the stereotype: I am obliged to make myself a lover, like everyone else: to be jealous, neglected,

R.H.

R.H.: Conversation.

frustrated, like everyone else. But when the relation is original, then the stereotype is shaken, transcended, evacuated, and jealousy, for instance, has no more room in this relation without a site, without *topos*—without what in French we call, colloquially, *"topo"*—without discourse.

Waiting

attente / waiting

Tumult of anxiety provoked by waiting for the
loved being, subject to trivial delays (rendezvous,
letters, telephone calls, returns).

1. I am waiting for an arrival, a return, a promised
sign. This can be futile, or immensely pathetic: in
Erwartung (*Waiting*), a woman waits for her lover, at
night, in the forest; I am waiting for no more than a
telephone call, but the anxiety is the same. Everything is
solemn: I have no sense of *proportions*.

Schönberg

2. There is a scenography of waiting: I organize it,
manipulate it, cut out a portion of time in which I shall
mime the loss of the loved object and provoke all the
effects of a minor mourning. This is then acted out as a
play.
The setting represents the interior of a café; we have a
rendezvous, I am waiting. In the Prologue, the sole actor
of the play (and with reason), I discern and indicate the
other's delay; this delay is as yet only a mathematical,
computable entity (I look at my watch several times); the
Prologue ends with a brainstorm: I decide to "take it
badly," I release the anxiety of waiting. Act I now begins;
it is occupied by suppositions: was there a misunderstand-
ing as to the time, the place? I try to recall the moment
when the rendezvous was made, the details which were
supplied. What is to be done (anxiety of behavior)? Try

another café? Telephone? But if the other comes during these absences? Not seeing me, the other might leave, etc. Act II is the act of anger; I address violent reproaches to the absent one: "All the same, he (she) could have . . ." "He (she) knows perfectly well . . ." Oh, if she (he) could be here, so that I could reproach her (him) for not being here! In Act III, I attain to (I obtain?) anxiety in the pure state: the anxiety of abandonment; I have just shifted in a second from absence to death; the other is as if dead: explosion of grief: I am internally *livid*. That is the play; it can be shortened by the other's arrival; if the other arrives in Act I, the greeting is calm; if the other arrives in Act II, there is a "scene"; if in Act II, there is recognition, the action of grace: I breathe deeply, like Pelléas emerging from the underground chambers and rediscovering life, the odor of roses.

Winnicott

Pelléas

(The anxiety of waiting is not continuously violent; it has its matte moments; I am waiting, and everything around my waiting is stricken with unreality: in this café, I look at the others who come in, chat, joke, read calmly: they are not waiting.)

3.   Waiting is an enchantment: I have received *orders not to move*. Waiting for a telephone call is thereby woven out of tiny unavowable interdictions *to infinity:* I forbid myself to leave the room, to go to the toilet, even to telephone (to keep the line from being busy); I suffer torments if someone else telephones me (for the same reason); I madden myself by the thought that at a certain (imminent) hour I shall have to leave, thereby running the risk of missing the healing call, the return of the

WINNICOTT: *Playing and Reality.*

Mother. All these diversions which solicit me are so many wasted moments for waiting, so many impurities of anxiety. For the anxiety of waiting, in its pure state, requires that I be sitting in a chair within reach of the telephone, without doing anything.

Winnicott

4.　　The being I am waiting for is not real. Like the mother's breast for the infant, "I create and re-create it over and over, starting from my capacity to love, starting from my need for it": the other comes here where I am waiting, here where I have already created him/her. And if the other does not come, I hallucinate the other: waiting is a delirium.

The telephone again: each time it rings, I snatch up the receiver, I think it will be the loved being who is calling me (since that being should call me); a little more effort and I "recognize" the other's voice, I engage in the dialogue, to the point where I lash out furiously against the importunate outsider who wakens me from my delirium. In the café, anyone who comes in, bearing the faintest resemblance, is thereupon, in a first impulse, *recognized*.

And, long after the amorous relation is allayed, I keep the habit of hallucinating the being I have loved: sometimes I am still in anxiety over a telephone call that is late, and no matter who is on the line, I imagine I recognize the voice I once loved: I am an amputee who still feels pain in his missing leg.

5.　　"Am I in love? —Yes, since I'm waiting." The other never waits. Sometimes I want to play the part of the

WINNICOTT: *Playing and Reality*.

one who doesn't wait; I try to busy myself elsewhere, to arrive late; but I always lose at this game: whatever I do, I find myself there, with nothing to do, punctual, even ahead of time. The lover's fatal identity is precisely: *I am the one who waits.*

(In transference, one always waits—at the doctor's, the professor's, the analyst's. Further, if I am waiting at a bank window, an airport ticket counter, I immediately establish an aggressive link with the teller, the stewardess, whose indifference unmasks and irritates my subjection; so that one might say that wherever there is waiting there is transference: I depend on a presence which is shared and requires time to be bestowed—as if it were a question of lowering my desire, lessening my need. *To make someone wait:* the constant prerogative of all power, "age-old pastime of humanity.")

E.B.

6.   A mandarin fell in love with a courtesan. "I shall be yours," she told him, "when you have spent a hundred nights waiting for me, sitting on a stool, in my garden, beneath my window." But on the ninety-ninth night, the mandarin stood up, put his stool under his arm, and went away.

E.B.: *Letter.*

Dark Glasses

cacher / to hide

A deliberative figure: the amorous subject
wonders, not whether he should declare his love
to the loved being (this is not a figure of avowal),
but to what degree he should conceal the
turbulences of his passion: his desires, his
distresses; in short, his excesses (in Racinian
language: his *fureur*).

1.   X, who left for his vacation without me, has shown
no signs of life since his departure: accident? post-office
strike? indifference? distancing maneuver? exercise of a
passing impulse of autonomy ("His youth deafens him, he
fails to hear")? or simple innocence? I grow increasingly
anxious, pass through each act of the waiting-scenario.
But when X reappears in one way or another, for he cannot fail to do so (a thought which should immediately
dispel any anxiety), what will I say to him? Should I hide
my distress—which will be over by then ("*How are
you?*")? Release it aggressively ("*That wasn't at all nice,
at least you could have . . .*") or passionately ("*Do you
know how much worry you caused me?*")? Or let this
distress of mine be delicately, discreetly understood, so
that it will be discovered without having to strike down the
other ("*I was rather concerned . . .*")? A secondary
anxiety seizes me, which is that I must determine the degree of publicity I shall give to my initial anxiety.

Mme de
Sévigné

2.   I am caught up in a double discourse, from which
I cannot escape. On the one hand, I tell myself: suppose

the other, by some arrangement of his own structure, needed my questioning? Then wouldn't I be justified in abandoning myself to the literal expression, the lyrical utterance of my "passion"? Are not excess and madness my truth, my strength? And if this truth, this strength ultimately prevailed?

But on the other hand, I tell myself: the signs of this passion run the risk of smothering the other. Then should I not, *precisely because of my love,* hide from the other how much I love him? I see the other with a double vision: sometimes as object, sometimes as subject; I hesitate between tyranny and oblation. Thus I doom myself to blackmail: if I love the other, I am forced to seek his happiness; but then I can only do myself harm: a trap: I am condemned to be a saint or a monster: unable to be the one, unwilling to be the other: hence I tergiversate: I show my passion a little.

Balzac

3.   To impose upon my passion the mask of discretion (of impassivity): this is a strictly heroic value: "It is unworthy of great souls to expose to those around them the distress they feel" (Clotilde de Vaux); Captain Paz, one of Balzac's heroes, invents a false mistress in order to be sure of keeping his best friend's wife from knowing that he loves her passionately.

Yet to hide a passion totally (or even to hide, more simply, its excess) is inconceivable: not because the human subject is too weak, but because passion is in essence made to be seen: the hiding must be seen: *I want you to know that I am hiding something from you,* that is the active paradox I must resolve: *at one and the same time* it must be known and not known: I want you to

BALZAC: *La Fausse maîtresse.*

know that I don't want to show my feelings: that is the message I address to the other. *Larvatus prodeo:* I advance pointing to my mask: I set a mask upon my passion, but with a discreet (and wily) finger I designate this mask. Every passion, ultimately, has its spectator: at the moment of his death, Captain Paz cannot keep from writing to the woman he has loved in silence: no amorous oblation without a final theater: the sign is always victorious.

4.　　Let us suppose that I have wept, on account of some incident of which the other has not even become aware (to weep is part of the normal activity of the amorous body), and that, *so this cannot be seen,* I put on dark glasses to mask my swollen eyes (a fine example of denial: to darken the sight in order not to be seen). The intention of this gesture is a calculated one: I want to keep the moral advantage of stoicism, of "dignity" (I take myself for Clotilde de Vaux), and at the same time, contradictorily, I want to provoke the tender question ("But what's the matter with you?"); I want to be both pathetic and admirable, I want to be at the same time a child and an adult. Thereby I gamble, I take a risk: for it is always possible that the other will simply ask no question whatever about these unaccustomed glasses; that the other will see, in the fact, no sign.

5.　　In order to suggest, delicately, that I am suffering, in order to hide without lying, I shall make use of a cunning preterition: I shall divide the economy of my signs. The task of the verbal signs will be to silence, to mask, to deceive: I shall never account, *verbally,* for the excesses of my sentiment. Having said nothing of the ravages of this anxiety, I can always, once it has passed, reassure myself that no one has guessed anything. The power of language: with my language I can do everything: even and especially *say nothing*.

I can do everything with my language, *but not with my body*. What I hide by my language, my body utters. I can deliberately mold my message, not my voice. By my voice, whatever it says, the other will recognize "that something is wrong with me." I am a liar (by preterition), not an actor. My body is a stubborn child, my language is a very civilized adult . . .

6.   . . . so that a long series of verbal contentions (my "politenesses") may suddenly explode into some generalized revulsion: a crying jag (for instance), before the other's flabbergasted eyes, will suddenly wipe out all the efforts (and the effects) of a carefully controlled language. I break apart:

Racine

> *Connais donc Phèdre et toute sa fureur.*
> Now you know Phaedra and all her fury.

"*Tutti Sistemati*"

casés / pigeonholed

The amorous subject sees everyone around him
as "pigeonholed," each appearing to be granted a
little practical and affective system of contractual
liaisons from which he feels himself to be
excluded; this inspires him with an ambiguous
sentiment of envy and mockery.

Werther

D.F.

1.　　Werther wants *to be pigeonholed:* "I . . . her
husband! O my God who created me, if you had kept this
happiness in store for me, all my life would be no more
than a perpetual thank offering," etc.: Werther wants a
place which is already taken—Albert's. He wants to enter
into a system ("pigeonholed," in Italian, is translated as
sistemato). For the system is a whole in which everyone
has his place (even if it is not a good place); husbands
and wives, lovers, trios, marginal figures as well (drugs,
cruising), nicely installed in their marginality: everyone
except me. (Game: there were as many chairs as children,
minus one; while the children marched around, a lady
pounded on a piano; when she stopped, everyone dashed
for a chair and sat down, except the clumsiest, the least
brutal, or the unluckiest, who remained standing, stupid,
de trop: the lover.)

2.　　How is it that the *sistemati* around me can inspire
me with envy? From what, seeing them, am I excluded?
Certainly not from a "dream," an "idyll," a "union":

D.F.: Conversation.

there are too many complaints from the "pigeonholed" about their system, and the dream of union forms another figure. No, what I fantasize in the system is quite modest (a fantasy all the more paradoxical in that it has no particular vividness): I want, I desire, quite simply, a *structure* (this word, lately, produced a gritting of teeth: it was regarded as the acme of abstraction). Of course there is not a happiness of structure; but every structure is *habitable,* indeed that may be its best definition. I can perfectly well inhabit what does not make me happy; I can simultaneously complain and endure; I can reject the meaning of the structure I submit to and traverse without displeasure certain of its everyday portions (habits, minor satisfactions, little securities, endurable things, temporary tensions); and I can even have a perverse liking for this behavior of the system (which makes it, in fact, habitable): Daniel Stylites lived quite well on top of his pillar: he had made it (though a difficult thing) into a structure.

To want to be pigeonholed is to want to obtain for life a docile reception. As support, the structure is separated from desire: what I want, quite simply, is to be "kept," like some sort of superior prostitute.

3.　　The other's structure (for the other always has a life structure to which I do not belong) has something absurd about it: I see the other insisting on living according to the same routines: kept elsewhere, the other seems to me frozen, *eternal* (eternity can be conceived as ridiculous).
· Each time I unexpectedly glimpsed the other in his "structure" (*sistemato*), I was fascinated: I believed I was contemplating an *essence:* that of conjugality. When the train

passes through the big cities of Holland on its high trestles, the traveler's gaze plunges down into the curtain-less, well-lighted interiors, where each person seems busy about his intimacy as if he were not being seen by thou-sands of passengers: that is when it is given to behold a Family essence; and when, in Hamburg, you walk along the streets of glass windows behind which women are smoking and waiting, it is the essence of Prostitution that you see. (Power of structures: perhaps that is what is desired in them.)

ESSENCE of P.

Catastrophe

catastrophe / catastrophe

Violent crisis during which the subject,
experiencing the amorous situation as a definitive
impasse, a trap from which he can never escape,
sees himself doomed to total destruction.

**Mlle de
Lespinasse**

1. Two systems of despair: gentle despair, active
resignation ("I love you as one must love, in despair"),
and violent despair: one day, after some incident, I shut
myself in my room and burst into sobs: I am carried away
by a powerful tide, asphyxiated with pain; my whole body
stiffens and convulses: I see, in a sharp, cold flash, the
destruction to which I am doomed. No relation to the
insidious and "civilized" depression of *amours difficiles;*
no relation to the fear and trembling of the abandoned
subject. This is clear as a catastrophe: *"I'm done for!"*

(Cause? Never formal—never by a declaration of breaking off; this comes without warning, either by the effect of
an unendurable image or by an abrupt sexual rejection:
the infantile—seeing oneself abandoned by the Mother—
shifts brutally to the genital.)

**Bruno
Bettelheim**

2. The amorous catastrophe may be close to what
has been called, in the psychotic domain, an *extreme
situation,* "a situation experienced by the subject as ir-
remediably bound to destroy him"; the image is drawn

BETTELHEIM: *The Empty Fortress.*

from what occurred at Dachau. Is it not indecent to compare the situation of a love-sick subject to that of an inmate of Dachau? Can one of the most unimaginable insults of History be compared with a trivial, childish, sophisticated, obscure incident occurring to a comfortable subject who is merely the victim of his own Image-repertoire? Yet these two situations have this in common: they are, literally, panic situations: situations without remainder, without return: I have projected myself into the other with such power that when I am without the other I cannot recover myself, regain myself: I am lost, forever.

etymology

F.W.

ETYMOLOGY: "Panic" relates to the god Pan; but we can play on etymologies as on words (as has always been done) and pretend to believe that "panic" comes from the Greek adjective that means "everything."
F.W.: Conversation.

Laetitia

circonscrire / to circumscribe

To reduce his wretchedness, the subject pins his
hope on a method of control which permits him to
circumscribe the pleasures afforded by the
amorous relation: on the one hand, to keep these
pleasures, to take full advantage of them, and on
the other hand, to place within a parenthesis of the
unthinkable those broad depressive zones which
separate such pleasures: "to forget" the loved
being outside of the pleasures that being bestows.

Leibnitz

1.   Cicero, and later Leibnitz, opposes *gaudium* to
laetitia. Gaudium is "the pleasure the soul experiences
when it considers the possession of a present or future
good as assured; and we are in possession of such a good
when it is in such a way within our power that we can
enjoy it when we wish." *Laetitia* is a lively pleasure, "a
state in which pleasure predominates within us" (among
other, often contradictory sensations).
Gaudium is what I dream of: to enjoy a lifelong pleasure.
But being unable to accede to *Gaudium,* from which I am
separated by a thousand obstacles, I dream of falling back
on *Laetitia:* if I could manage to confine myself to the
lively pleasures the other affords me, without contaminat-
ing them, mortifying them by the anxiety which serves as
their hinge? If I could take an anthological view of the
amorous relation? If I were to understand, initially, that a
great preoccupation does not exclude moments of pure
pleasure (like the Chaplain in *Mother Courage* explaining

LEIBNITZ: *New Essays on Human Understanding.*

Brecht that "war does not exclude peace"), and then, if I managed systematically to forget the zones of alarm which separate these moments of pleasure? If I could be dazed, inconsistent?

2.   This is a lunatic project, for the Image-repertoire is *precisely* defined by its coalescence (its adhesiveness), or again: its power of association: nothing in the image can be forgotten; an exhausting memory forbids *voluntarily* escaping love; in short, forbids inhabiting it discreetly, reasonably. I can certainly imagine procedures to obtain the circumscription of my pleasures (converting the scarcity of frequentation into the luxury of the relation, in the Epicurean fashion; or again, considering the other as lost, and henceforth enjoying, each time the other returns, the relief of a resurrection), but it is a waste of effort: the amorous *glue* is indissoluble; one must either submit or cut loose: accommodation is impossible (love is neither dialectical nor reformist).

(A melancholy version of the circumscription of pleasures: my life is a ruin: some things remain in place, others are dissolved, collapsed: this is dilapidation, wreckage.)

BRECHT: *Mother Courage*, scene vi.

The Heart

coeur / heart

This word refers to all kinds of movements and
desires, but what is constant is that the heart is
constituted into a gift-object—whether ignored
or rejected.

1.   The heart is the organ of desire (the heart swells,
weakens, etc., like the sexual organs), as it is held, enchanted, within the domain of the Image-repertoire. What
will the world, what will the other do with my desire? That
is the anxiety in which are gathered all the heart's movements, all the heart's "problems."

Werther

2.   Werther complains of Prince von X: "He esteems
my mind and my talents more than this heart of mine,
which yet is my one pride . . . Ah, whatever I know,
anyone may know—I alone have my heart."
You wait for me where I do not want to go: you love me
where I do not exist. Or again: the world and I are not
interested in the same thing; and to my misfortune, this
divided thing is myself; I am not interested (Werther
says) in my mind; you are not interested in my heart.

3.   The heart is what I imagine I give. Each time this
gift is returned to me, then it is little enough to say, with
Werther, that the heart is what remains of me, once all the
wit attributed to me and undesired by me is taken away:

the heart is what remains *to me,* and this heart that lies heavy on my heart is heavy with the ebb which has filled it with itself (only the lover and the child have a heavy heart).

(X is about to leave for some weeks, and perhaps longer; at the last moment, he wants to buy a watch for his trip; the clerk simpers at him: "Would you like mine? You would have been a little boy when they cost what this one did," etc.; she doesn't know that *my heart is heavy within me.*)

"All the delights of the earth"

comblement / fulfillment

The subject insistently posits the desire and the possibility of a complete satisfaction of the desire implicated in the amorous relation and of a perfect and virtually eternal success of this relation: paradisiac image of the Sovereign Good, to be given and to be received.

1.   "Now, take all the delights of the earth, melt them into one single delight, and cast it entire into a single man—all this will be as nothing to the delight of which I speak." Thus fulfillment is a precipitation: something is condensed, streams over me, strikes me like a lightning bolt. What is it which fills me in this fashion? A totality? No. Something that, starting from totality, actually exceeds it: a totality without remainder, a *summa* without exception, a site with nothing adjacent ("my soul is not only filled, but runs over"). I fulfill (I am fulfilled), I accumulate, but I do not abide by the level of lack; I produce an *excess,* and it is in this excess that the fulfillment occurs (the excessive is the realm, the system of the Image-repertoire: once I am no longer within the excessive, I feel frustrated; for me, *enough* means *not enough*): at last I know that state in which "delight exceeds the possibilities envisioned by desire." A miracle: leaving all "satisfaction" behind, neither satiated nor drunk (*saoul,*

Ruysbroeck

Ruysbroeck

etymology

ETYMOLOGY: *Satis* (enough), in both "satisfaction" and *"saoul"* (*satullus*).

in French), I pass beyond the limits of satiety, and instead of finding disgust, nausea or even drunkenness, I discover . . . *Coincidence.* Excess has led me to proportion; I adhere to the Image, our proportions are the same: exactitude, accuracy, music: I am through with *not enough.* Henceforth I live in the definitive assumption of the Image-repertoire, its triumph.

Fulfillments: they are not spoken—so that, erroneously, the amorous relation seems reduced to a long complaint. This is because, if it is inconsistent to express suffering badly, on the other hand, with regard to happiness, it would seem culpable to spoil its expression: the ego discourses only when it is hurt; when I am fulfilled or remember having been so, language seems pusillanimous: I am *transported,* beyond language, i.e., beyond the mediocre, beyond the general: "There occurs an encounter which is intolerable, on account of the joy within it, and sometimes man is thereby reduced to nothing; this is what I call the transport. The transport is the joy of which one cannot speak."

Ruysbroeck

2.   In reality, it is unimportant that I have no likelihood of being *really* fulfilled (I am quite willing for this to be the case). Only the will to fulfillment shines, indestructible, before me. By this will, I well up: I form within myself the utopia of a subject free from repression: I am this subject *already*. This subject is libertarian: to believe in the Sovereign Good is as insane as to believe in the Sovereign Evil: Heinrich von Ofterdingen is of the same philosophical stuff as Sade's Juliette.

Novalis

Nietzsche

(Fulfillment means an abolition of inheritances: ". . . Joy has no need of heirs or of children—Joy wants itself, wants eternity, the repetition of the same things, wants everything to remain eternally the same." The fulfilled lover has no need to write, to transmit, to reproduce.)

"I have an Other-ache"

compassion / compassion

The subject experiences a sentiment of violent
compassion with regard to the loved object each
time he sees, feels, or knows the loved object is
unhappy or in danger, for whatever reason
external to the amorous relation itself.

1.   "Supposing that we experienced the other as he
experiences himself—which Schopenhauer calls *compassion* and which might more accurately be called a union
within suffering, a unity of suffering—we should hate the
other when he himself, like Pascal, finds himself hateful."
If the other suffers from hallucinations, if he fears going
mad, I should myself hallucinate, myself go mad. Now,
whatever the power of love, this does not occur: I am
moved, anguished, for it is horrible to see those one loves
suffering, but at the same time I remain dry, watertight.
My identification is imperfect: I am a Mother (the other
causes me concern), but an insufficient Mother; I bestir
myself too much, in proportion to the profound reserve in
which, actually, I remain. For at the same time that I
"sincerely" identify myself with the other's misery, what I
read in this misery is that it occurs *without me,* and that
by being miserable by himself, the other abandons me: if
he suffers without my being the cause of his suffering, it is
because I don't count for him: his suffering annuls me
insofar as it constitutes him outside of myself.

Nietzsche

Michelet

NIETZSCHE: *The Dawn.*
MICHELET: Saying, "I have a France-ache."

2.   Whereupon, a reversal: since the other suffers
without me, why suffer in his place? His misery bears him
far away from me, I can only exhaust myself running after
him, without ever hoping to be able to catch up, to coincide with him. So let us become a little detached, let us
undertake the apprenticeship of a certain distance. Let the
repressed word appear which rises to the lips of every
subject, once he survives another's death: *Let us live!*

3.   So I shall suffer with the other, but *without pressure,* without losing myself. Such behavior, at once very
affective and very controlled, very amorous and very
civilized, can be given a name: *delicacy:* in a sense it is the
"healthy" (artistic) form of compassion. (Ate is the
goddess of madness, but Plato speaks of Ate's delicacy:
her foot is winged, it touches lightly.)

Symposium

"I want to understand"

comprendre / **to understand**
Suddenly perceiving the amorous episode as a knot
of inexplicable reasons and impaired solutions, the
subject exclaims: "I want to understand (what is
happening to me)!"

1.　　What do I think of love? —As a matter of fact, I
think nothing at all of love. I'd be glad to know *what it is,*
but being inside, I see it in existence, not in essence. What
I want to know (love) is the very substance I employ in
order to speak (the lover's discourse). Reflection is certainly permitted, but since this reflection is immediately
absorbed in the mulling over of images, it never turns into
reflexivity: excluded from logic (which supposes languages exterior to each other), I cannot claim *to think
properly.* Hence, discourse on love though I may for years
at a time, I cannot hope to seize the concept of it except
"by the tail": by flashes, formulas, surprises of expression,
scattered through the great stream of the Image-repertoire;
I am in love's *wrong place,* which is its dazzling place:
"The darkest place, according to a Chinese proverb, is
always underneath the lamp."

Reik

2.　　Coming out of the movie theater, alone, mulling
over my "problem," my lover's problem which the film

REIK: Quoted in *Fragments of a Great Confession.*

has been unable to make me forget, I utter this strange cry: not: *make it stop!* but: *I want to understand* (what is happening to me)!

3.   Repression: I want to analyze, to know, to express in another language than mine; I want to represent my delirium to myself, I want to "look in the face" what is dividing me, cutting me off. *Understand your madness:* that was Zeus' command when he ordered Apollo to turn the faces of the divided Androgynes (like an egg, a berry) toward the place where they had been cut apart (the belly) "so that the sight of their division might render them less insolent." To understand—is that not to divide the image, to undo the *I,* proud organ of misapprehension?

Symposium

4.   Interpretation: no, that is not what your cry means. As a matter of fact, that cry is still a cry of love: "I want to understand myself, to make myself understood, make myself known, be embraced; I want someone to take me with him." That is what your cry means.

A.C.

5.   I want to change systems: no longer to unmask, no longer to interpret, but to make consciousness itself a drug, and thereby to accede to the perfect vision of reality, to the great bright dream, to prophetic love.
(And if consciousness—such consciousness—were our human future? If, by an additional turn of the spiral, some day, most dazzling of all, once every reactive ideology had

etymology

A.C.: Letter.
ETYMOLOGY: The Greeks opposed ὄναρ (*onar*), the vulgar dream, to ὕπαρ (*hypar*), the prophetic (never believed) vision. Communicated by J.-L.B.

disappeared, consciousness were finally to become this: the abolition of the manifest and the latent, of the appearance and the hidden? If it were asked of analysis not to destroy power (not even to correct or to direct it), but only *to decorate* it, as an artist? Let us imagine that the science of our *lapsi* were to discover, one day, its own *lapsus,* and that this *lapsus* should turn out to be: a new, unheard-of form of consciousness?)

"*What is to be done?*"

conduite / behavior

A deliberative figure: the amorous subject raises
(generally) futile problems of behavior: faced
with this or that alternative, what is to be done?
How is he to act?

Werther

1.   Should one continue? Wilhelm, Werther's friend, is
the man of Ethics, the unpersuadable science of behavior.
This ethic is actually a kind of logic: either this or else
that; if I choose (if I determine) this, then once again, this
or that: and so on, until, from this cascade of alternatives,
appears at last a pure action—pure of all regret, all vacillation. You love Charlotte: *either you have some hope,
and then you will act; or else you have none, in which
case you will renounce.* That is the discourse of the
"healthy" subject: *either / or.* But the amorous subject
replies (as Werther does): I am trying to slip between
the two members of the alternative: i.e., *I have no hope,
but all the same . . .* Or else: I stubbornly choose not
to choose; I choose drifting: *I continue.*

2.   My anxieties as to behavior are futile, ever more
so, to infinity. If the other, incidentally or negligently,
gives the telephone number of a place where he or she can
be reached at certain times, I immediately grow baffled:
should I telephone or shouldn't I? (It would do no good to
tell me that *I can* telephone—that is the objective, reasonable meaning of the message—for it is precisely this *per-
mission* I don't know how to handle.)

What is futile is what apparently has and will have no consequence. But for me, an amorous subject, everything which is new, everything which disturbs, is received not as a fact but in the aspect of a sign which must be interpreted. From the lover's point of view, the fact becomes consequential because it is immediately transformed into a sign: it is the sign, not the fact, which is consequential (by its *aura*). If the other has given me this new telephone number, what was that the sign of? Was it an invitation to telephone *right away,* for the pleasure of the call, or only *should the occasion arise,* out of necessity? My answer itself will be a sign, which the other will inevitably interpret, thereby releasing, between us, a tumultuous maneuvering of images. *Everything signifies:* by this proposition, I entrap myself, I bind myself in calculations, I keep myself from enjoyment.

Sometimes, by dint of deliberating about "nothing" (as the world sees it), I exhaust myself; then I try, in reaction, to return—like a drowning man who stamps on the floor of the sea—to a *spontaneous* decision (spontaneity: the great dream: paradise, power, delight): *go on, telephone, since you want to!* But such recourse is futile: amorous time does not permit the subject to align impulse and action, to make them coincide: I am not the man of mere "acting out"—my madness is tempered, it is not seen; it is *right away* that I fear consequences, any consequence: it is my fear—my deliberation—which is "spontaneous."

3.   *Karma* is the (disastrous) concatenation of actions (of their causes and their effects). The Buddhist

Zen

wants to withdraw from karma; to suspend the play of causality; he wants to vacate the signs, to ignore the practical question: what is to be done? I cannot stop asking it, and I sigh after that suspension of karma which is *nirvana*. Hence the situations which happen to impose no responsibility for behavior upon me, however painful, are received in a sort of peace; I suffer, but at least I have nothing to decide; the amorous (imaginary) machinery here operates all by itself, within me; like a workman of the electronic age, or like the dunce in the last row of the classroom, all I have to do is *be there:* karma (the machinery, the classroom) functions in front of me, but without me. In misery itself, I can, for a very brief interval, devise for myself a *little corner of sloth.*

Connivance

connivence / connivance

The subject imagines himself speaking about the
loved being with a rival person, and this image
generates and strangely develops in him a pleasure
of complicity.

1.　　The person with whom I can in fact talk about the
loved being is the person who loves that being as much as
I do, the way I do: my symmetric partner, my rival, my
competitor (rivalry is a question of place). I can then, for
once, discuss the other *with someone who knows;* there
occurs an equality of knowledge, a delight of inclusion; in
such discussion, the object is neither distanced nor
lacerated; it remains interior to and protected by the dual
discourse. I coincide simultaneously with the Image and
with this second mirror which reflects what I am (on the
rival countenance, it is my fear, my jealousy which I
read). Bustling gossip, all jealousy suspended, around this
absent party whose objective nature is reinforced by two
converging visions: we give ourselves over to a rigorous,
successful experiment, since there are two observers and
since the two observations are made under the same con-
ditions: the object is *proved:* I discover that *I am right* (to
be happy, to be injured, to be anxious).

etymology (Connivance: *connivere:* means at one and the same time:
I wink, I blink, I close my eyes.)

2.　　Which brings us to this paradox: it is the loved
being who, in the triune relation, is virtually *de trop*. This

can be read in certain *awkwardnesses*. When the loved object happens to complain of my rival, disparages him, I don't know how to reply to this complaint: on the one hand, it is "noble" not to take advantage of a confidence which is useful to me—which seems to "reinforce" my situation; and on the other hand, I am cautious: I know that I occupy the same position as my rival and that, therefore, all psychology, all value set aside, nothing can keep me as well from being, one day, the object of disparagement. And sometimes it is I myself who praise my rival to the loved being (in order to be "generous"?) against which the loved being, strangely enough (in order to flatter me?), protests.

3.   Jealousy is an equation involving three permutable (indeterminable) terms: one is always jealous of two persons at once: I am jealous of the one I love and of the one who loves the one I love. The *odiosamato* (as the Italians call the "rival") is *also* loved by me: he interests me, intrigues me, appeals to me (see Dostoevsky's *Eternal Husband*).

D.F.

D.F.: Conversation.

"When my finger accidentally . . ."

contacts / contacts

The figure refers to any interior discourse provoked by a furtive contact with the body (and more precisely the skin) of the desired being.

Werther

1. Accidentally, Werther's finger touches Charlotte's, their feet, under the table, happen to brush against each other. Werther might be engrossed by the meaning of these accidents; he might concentrate physically on these slight zones of contact and delight in this fragment of inert finger or foot, fetishistically, *without concern for the response* (like God—as the etymology of the word tells us—the Fetish does not reply). But in fact Werther is not perverse, he is in love: he creates meaning, always and everywhere, out of nothing, and it is meaning which thrills him: he is in the crucible of meaning. Every contact, for the lover, raises the question of an answer: the skin is asked to reply.

(A squeeze of the hand—enormous documentation—a tiny gesture within the palm, a knee which doesn't move away, an arm extended, as if quite naturally, along the back of a sofa and against which the other's head gradually comes to rest—this is the paradisiac realm of subtle and clandestine signs: a kind of festival not of the senses but of meaning.)

2.   Charlus takes the narrator's chin and slides his
magnetized fingers up to the ears "like a barber's fingers."
This trivial gesture, which I begin, is continued by another
part of myself; without anything interrupting it physically,
it branches off, shifts from a simple function to a dazzling
meaning, that of the demand for love. Meaning (destiny)
electrifies my hand; I am about to tear open the other's
opaque body, oblige the other (whether there is a response, a withdrawal, or mere acceptance) to enter into
the interplay of meaning: I am about *to make the other
speak.* In the lover's realm, there is no *acting out:* no
propulsion, perhaps even no pleasure—nothing but signs,
a frenzied activity of language: to institute, on each
furtive occasion, the system (the paradigm) of demand
and response.

PROUST: *The Guermantes' Way.*

Events, Setbacks, Annoyances

contingences / contingencies

Trivialities, incidents, setbacks, pettinesses, irritations, the vexations of amorous existence; any factual nucleus whose consequences intersect the amorous subject's will to happiness, as if chance conspired against him.

1.　"Because, this morning, X was in a good mood, because I received a present from X, because our next meeting is all set—but because, unexpectedly, tonight, I ran into X accompanied by Y, because I imagined them whispering together about me when they caught sight of me, because this meeting has demonstrated the ambiguity of our situation, and perhaps even X's duplicity—the euphoria has stopped."

2.　The incident is trivial (it is always trivial) but it will attract to it whatever language I possess. I immediately transform it into an important event, *devised* by something which resembles fate. It is a covering which falls over me, enveloping everything. Countless minor circumstances thus weave the black veil of Maya, the tapestry of illusions, of meanings, of words. I begin *classifying* what happens to me. The incident will now produce an irritation, like the pea under the princess's twenty mattresses; like one of the day's thoughts swarming in a

Andersen

Freud

dream, it will be the instigator of the lover's discourse, which will reproduce and multiply by means of the Image-repertoire's capital.

3. In the incident, it is not the cause which pulls me up short and which echoes within me thereupon, but the structure. The entire structure of the relation comes to me as one might pull a tablecloth toward one: its disadvantages, its snares, its impasses (similarly, in the tiny lens embellishing the mother-of-pearl penholder, I could see Paris and the Eiffel Tower). I make no recriminations, develop no suspicions, search for no causes; I see in terror the *scope* of the situation in which I am caught up; I am not the man of resentment, but of fatality.

(For me, the incident is a sign, not an index: the element of a system, not the efflorescence of a causality.)

4. Sometimes, hysterically, my own body produces the incident: an evening I was looking forward to with delight, a heartfelt declaration whose effect, I felt, would be highly beneficial—these I obstruct by a stomach ache, an attack of grippe: all the possible substitutes of hysterical aphonia.

FREUD: *The Interpretation of Dreams.*

The Other's Body

corps / body
Any thought, any feeling, any interest aroused in
the amorous subject by the loved body.

1.   The other's body was divided: on one side, the
body proper—skin, eyes—tender, warm; and on the other
side, the voice—abrupt, reserved, subject to fits of
remoteness, a voice which did not give what the body
gave. Or further: on one side, the soft, warm, downy,
adorable body, and on the other, the ringing, well-formed,
worldly voice—always the voice.

2.   Sometimes an idea occurs to me: I catch myself
carefully scrutinizing the loved body (like the narrator
watching Albertine asleep). *To scrutinize* means *to
search:* I am searching the other's body, as if I wanted to
see what was inside it, as if the mechanical cause of my
desire were in the adverse body (I am like those children
who take a clock apart in order to find out what time is).
This operation is conducted in a cold and astonished
fashion; I am calm, attentive, as if I were confronted by a
strange insect of which I am suddenly *no longer afraid.*
Certain parts of the body are particularly appropriate to
this *observation:* eyelashes, nails, roots of the hair, the
incomplete objects. It is obvious that I am then in the
process of fetishizing a corpse. As is proved by the fact
that if the body I am scrutinizing happens to emerge from
its inertia, if it begins *doing something,* my desire changes;

Proust

if for instance I see the other *thinking,* my desire ceases to be perverse, it again becomes imaginary, I return to an Image, to a Whole: once again, I love.

(I was looking at everything in the other's face, the other's body, coldly: lashes, toenail, thin eyebrows, thin lips, the luster of the eyes, a mole, a way of holding a cigarette; I was fascinated—fascination being, after all, only the extreme of detachment—by a kind of colored ceramicized, vitrified figurine in which I could read, without understanding anything about it, *the cause of my desire.*)

Talking

déclaration / declaration

The amorous subject's propensity to talk copiously,
with repressed feeling, to the loved being, about
his love for that being, for himself, for them: the
declaration does not bear upon the avowal of love,
but upon the endlessly glossed form of the
amorous relation.

1.   Language is a skin: I rub my language against the
other. It is as if I had words instead of fingers, or fingers at
the tip of my words. My language trembles with desire.
The emotion derives from a double contact: on the one
hand, a whole activity of discourse discreetly, indirectly
focuses upon a single signified, which is "I desire you,"
and releases, nourishes, ramifies it to the point of explosion (language experiences orgasm upon touching itself);
on the other hand, I enwrap the other in my words, I
caress, brush against, talk up this contact, I extend myself
to make the commentary to which I submit the relation
endure.

(To speak amorously is to expend without an end in sight,
without a *crisis;* it is to practice a relation without orgasm.
There may exist a literary form of this *coitus reservatus:*
what we call Marivaudage.)

2.   The energy of commentary shifts, follows the path
of substitutions. Initially it is for the other that I discourse

upon the relation; but this may also occur in the presence of my confidant: from *you* I shift to *he* or *she*. And then, from *he* or *she* I shift to *one:* I elaborate an abstract discourse about love, a philosophy of the thing, which would then in fact be nothing but a generalized suasion. Retracing our steps from here, one might say that every discussion of love (however detached its tonality) inevitably involves a secret allocution (I am addressing someone whom you do not know but who is there, at the end of my maxims). In the *Symposium,* we may find this allocution: it may well be Agathon whom Alcibiades is addressing and whom he desires, though he is being monitored by an analyst, Socrates.

Lacan

(Love's atopia, the characteristic which causes it to escape all dissertations, would be that *ultimately* it is possible to talk about love only *according to a strict allocutive determination;* whether philosophical, gnomic, lyric, or novelistic, there is always, in the discourse upon love, a person whom one addresses, though this person may have shifted to the condition of a phantom or a creature still to come. No one wants to speak of love unless it is *for* someone.)

The Dedication

dédicace / dedication

An episode of language which accompanies any
amorous gift, whether real or projected; and, more
generally, every gesture, whether actual or
interior, by which the subject dedicates something
to the loved being.

1.   The amorous gift is sought out, selected, and pur-
chased in the greatest excitement—the kind of excitement
which seems to be of the order of orgasm. Strenuously I
calculate whether this object will give pleasure, whether it
will disappoint, or whether, on the contrary, seeming too
"important," it will in and of itself betray the delirium—
or the snare in which I am caught. The amorous gift is a
solemn one; swept away by the devouring metonymy
which governs the life of the imagination, I transfer myself
inside it altogether. By this object, I give you my All, I
touch you with my phallus; it is for this reason that I am
mad with excitement, that I rush from shop to shop, stubbornly tracking down the "right" fetish, the brilliant, successful fetish which will *perfectly* suit your desire.

The gift is contact, sensuality: you will be touching what I
have touched, a third skin unites us. I give X a scarf and
he wears it: X *gives* me the fact of wearing it; and,
moreover, this is how he, naïvely, conceives and speaks of
the phenomenon. *A contrario:* any ethic of purity requires
that we detach the gift from the hand which gives or receives it: in Buddhist ordination, personal objects and the
three garments are offered to the bonze on a pole; the
bonze accepts them by touching them with a stick, not

with his hand; thus, in the future, everything which will be given to him—and on which he will live—will be arranged on a table, on the ground, or on a fan.

2.   I have this fear: that the given object may not function properly because of some insidious defect: if it is a box (selected very carefully), for example, the latch doesn't work (the shop being run by society women; and, moreover, the shop is called *"Because I love"*—is it *because I love* that the latch doesn't work?). The delight of giving the present then evaporates, and the subject knows that whatever he gives, he does not have it.

(One does not give merely an object: X being in analysis, Y wants to be analyzed too: analysis as a gift of love?)

The gift is not necessarily excrement, but it has, nonetheless, a vocation as waste: the gift I receive is more than I know what to do with, it does not fit my space, it encumbers, it is too much: "What am I going to do with your present!"

3.   A typical argument of a "scene" is to represent to the other what you are giving him or her (time, energy, money, ingenuity, other relations, etc.); for it is invoking the reply which makes any scene "move": *And what about me! Haven't I given you everything?* The gift then reveals the test of strength of which it is the instrument: "I'll give you more than you give me, and so I will dominate you" (in the great Indian potlatches, whole villages were burned, slaves slaughtered with this intention).

To declare what I am giving is to follow the family model: *look at the sacrifices we're making for you;* or again: *we*

PH.S.: Conversation.

gave you the gift of life (—But what the fuck do I care about life! etc.). To speak of the gift is to place it in an exchange economy (of sacrifice, competition, etc.); which stands opposed to silent expenditure.

Symposium

R.H.

4.   "To that god, O Phaedrus, I dedicate this discourse . . ." One cannot give language (how to transfer it from one hand to the other?), but one can dedicate it—since the other is a minor god. The given object is reabsorbed in the sumptuous, solemn utterance of the consecration, in the poetic gesture of the dedication; the gift is exalted in the very voice which expresses it, if this voice is *measured* (metrical); or again: *sung* (lyrical); this is the very principle of the *Hymn* or *Anthem.* Being unable to give anything, I dedicate the dedication itself, into which is absorbed all I have to say:

Baudelaire

> *A la très chère, à la très belle,*
> *Qui remplit mon coeur de clarté,*
> *A l'ange, à l'idole immortelle . . .*
> To the beloved, the beautiful being
> who fills my heart with light, to
> the angel, the immortal idol . . .

Song is the precious addition to a blank message, entirely contained within its address, for what I give by singing is at once my body (by my voice) and the silence into which you cast that body. (Love is mute, Novalis says; only poetry makes it speak.) *Song means nothing:* it is in this that you will understand at last what it is that I give you; as useless as the wisp of yarn, the pebble held out to his mother by the child.

5.   Powerless to utter itself, powerless to speak, love

R.H.: Conversation.

nonetheless wants to proclaim itself, to exclaim, to write itself everywhere: *all'acqua, all'ombra, ai monti, ai fiori, all'erbe, ai fonti, all'eco, all'aria, ai venti* . . . And once the amorous subject creates or puts together any kind of work at all, he is seized with a desire to dedicate it. What he makes he immediately, and even in advance, wants to give to his beloved, for whom he has worked, or will work. The addition of the name will take its place as a way of uttering the gift.

Yet, except for the case of the Hymn, which combines the dedication and the text itself, what follows the dedication (i.e., the work itself) has little relation to this dedication. The object I give is no longer tautological (I give you what I give you), it is *interpretable;* it has a meaning (meanings) greatly in excess of its address; though I write your name on my work, it is for "them" that it has been written (the others, the readers). Hence it is by a fatality of writing itself that we cannot say of a text that it is "amorous," but only, at best, that it has been created "amorously," like a cake or an embroidered slipper.

And even: less than a slipper! For the slipper has been made for your foot (your size and your pleasure); the cake has been made or selected for your taste: there is a certain adequation between these objects and your person. But writing does not possess this obligingness. Writing is dry, obtuse; a kind of steamroller, writing advances, indifferent, indelicate, and would kill "father, mother, lover" rather than deviate from its fatality (enigmatic though that fatality may be). When I write, I must acknowledge this fact (which, according to my Image-repertoire, lacerates me): there is no benevolence within writing, rather a terror: it smothers the other, who, far from perceiving the gift in it, reads there instead an assertion of mastery, of

The Marriage of Figaro: Cherubino's aria (Act I).

power, of pleasure, of solitude. Whence the cruel paradox
of the dedication: I seek at all costs to give you what
smothers you.

(We often notice that a writing subject does not have his
writing "in his own image": if you love me "for myself,"
you do not love me for my writing (and I suffer from it).
Doubtless, loving simultaneously two signifiers in the same
body is too much! It doesn't happen every day—and if it
should happen, by some exception, that is Coincidence,
the Sovereign Good.)

6.   Hence I cannot give you what I thought I was
writing for you—that is what I must acknowledge: the
amorous dedication is impossible (I shall not be satisfied
with a worldly or mundane signature, pretending to dedicate to you a work which escapes us both). The operation
in which the other is to be engaged is not a signature. It is,
more profoundly, an inscription: the other is inscribed, he
inscribes himself within the text, he leaves there his (multiple) traces. If you were only the dedicatee of this book,
you would not escape your harsh condition as (loved)
object—as god; but your presence within the text,
whereby you are unrecognizable there, is not that of an
analogical figure, of a fetish, but that of a force which is
not, thereby, absolutely reliable. Hence it doesn't matter
that you feel continuously reduced to silence, that your
own discourse seems to you smothered beneath the
monstrous discourse of the amorous subject: in *Teorema*
the "other" does not speak, but he inscribes something
within each of those who desire him—he performs what
the mathematicians call a catastrophe (the disturbance of
one system by another): it is true that this mute figure is
an angel.

Pasolini

"We are our own demons"

démons / demons

> It occasionally seems to the amorous subject that
> he is possessed by a demon of language which
> impels him to injure himself and to expel
> himself—according to Goethe's expression—from
> the paradise which at other moments the amorous
> relation constitutes for him.

1.   A specific force impels my language toward the
harm I may do to myself: the motor system of my discourse is the wheel *out of gear:* language snowballs, without any tactical thought of reality. I seek to harm myself, I
expel myself from my paradise, busily provoking within
myself the images (of jealousy, abandonment, humilia-
tion) which can injure me; and I keep the wound open, I
feed it with other images, until another wound appears
and produces a diversion.

Goethe

2.   The demon is plural ("My name is Legion," Mark
5:9). When a demon is repulsed, when I have at last
imposed silence upon him (by accident or effort), another
raises his head close by and begins speaking. The demonic
life of a lover is like the surface of a solfatara; huge
bubbles (muddy and scorching) burst, one after the other;
when one falls back and dies out, returning to the mass,

GOETHE: "We are our own demons, we expel ourselves from our
paradise" (*Werther*, notes).

another forms and swells farther on. The bubbles "Despair," "Jealousy," "Exclusion," "Desire," "Uncertainty of Behavior," "Fear of Losing Face" (the nastiest of all the demons) explode in an indeterminate order, one after the next: the very *disorder* of Nature.

3.   How to repulse a demon (an old problem)? The demons, especially if they are demons of language (and what else could they be?) are fought by language. Hence I can hope to exorcise the demonic word which is breathed into my ears (by myself) if I substitute for it (if I have the gifts of language for doing so) another, calmer word (I yield to euphemism). Thus: I imagined I had escaped from the crisis at last, when behold—favored by a long car trip—a flood of language sweeps me away, I keep tormenting myself with the thought, desire, regret, and rage of the other; and I add to these wounds the discouragement of having to acknowledge that *I am falling back,* relapsing; but the French vocabulary is a veritable pharmacopoeia (poison on one side, antidote on the other): no, this is not a relapse, only a last *soubresaut,* a final convulsion of the previous demon.

Domnei

dépendance / dependency

A figure in which common opinion sees the very
condition of the amorous subject, subjugated to
the loved object.

1. The mechanics of amorous vassalage require a
fathomless futility. For, in order that dependency be manifest in all its purity, it must burst forth in the most trivial
circumstances and become inadmissible by dint of
cowardice: waiting for a phone call is somehow too crude
a dependency; I must improve upon it, without limits:
hence I shall exasperate myself with the chatter of the
women in the drugstore who are delaying my return to the
instrument to which I am subjugated; and since this call,
which I don't want to miss, will bring me some new occasion for subjugation, it is as if I were energetically behaving in order to preserve the very space of dependency, in
order to permit this dependency to function: I am distracted by dependency, but even more—a further complication—I am humiliated by this distraction.

cortezia
Symposium

(If I acknowledge my dependency, I do so because for me
it is a means of *signifying* my demand: in the realm of
love, futility is not a "weakness" or an "absurdity": it is a
strong sign: the more futile, the more it signifies and the
more it asserts itself as strength.)

CORTEZIA: Courtly love is based on amorous vassalage (*Domnei* or
Donnoi).

2.   The other is assigned to a superior habitat, an Olympus where everything is decided and whence everything descends upon me. These descents of decisions are sometimes staggered, for the other, too, may be subject to an instance beyond his powers, so that I am twice subject: to the one I love and to *his* dependency. That is when I begin to baulk; for the higher decision of which I am the last and somehow deflated object now seems to me altogether unfair: I am no more in Fatality than as a good tragic subject I had chosen myself. I am delivered up to that historical stage where aristocratic power begins to undergo the first effects of democratic demands: *"No reason that I should be the one who,"* etc.

(The choice of vacation, with its complicated calendar, in whatever network I find myself participating, wonderfully favors these first demands.)

Exuberance

dépense / expenditure

A figure by which the amorous subject both seeks
and hesitates to place love in an economy of
pure expenditure, of "total loss."

Werther

1.   Albert, a flat, ethical, conformist character,
decrees (after how many others) that suicide is a form of
cowardice. For Werther, on the contrary, suicide is not a
weakness, since it issues from a tension: "Oh, my dear
friend, if to tender one's whole being is to give evidence of
strength why should an excessive tension be weakness?"
Love-as-passion is therefore a force, a strength ("this violence, this stubborn, indomitable passion"), something
which suggests the old notion of ἰσχύς (*ischus:* energy, tension, strength of character), and, closer to us, that of
Expenditure.

Greek

(This must be remembered if we would glimpse the trans-
gressive force of love-as-passion: the assumption of sentimentality as alien strength.)

Werther

2.   In Werther, at a certain moment, two economies
are opposed. On the one hand, there is the young lover
who lavishes his time, his faculties, his fortune without
counting the cost; on the other, there is the philistine (the
petty official) who moralizes to him: "Parcel out your
time . . . Calculate your fortune," etc. On the one hand,

GREEK: A Stoic notion.

there is the lover Werther who expends his love every day, without any sense of saving or of compensation, and on the other, there is the husband Albert, who economizes his goods, his happiness. On the one hand, a bourgeois economy of repletion; on the other, a perverse economy of dispersion, of waste, of frenzy (*furor wertherinus*).

(A British lord, and subsequently a bishop, blamed Goethe for the epidemic of suicides provoked by *Werther*. To which Goethe replied in strictly *economic* terms: "Your commercial system has claimed thousands of victims, why not grant a few to *Werther?*")

3.　　The lover's discourse is not lacking in calculations: I rationalize, I reason, sometimes I count, either to obtain certain satisfactions, to avoid certain injuries, or to represent inwardly to the other, in a wayward impulse, the wealth of ingenuity I lavish *for nothing* in his favor (to yield, to conceal, not to hurt, to divert, to convince, etc.). But these calculations are merely impatiences: no thought of a final gain: Expenditure is open, to infinity, strength drifts, without a goal (the loved object is not a goal: the loved object is an object-as-thing, not an object-as-term).

4.　　When amorous Expenditure is continuously affirmed, without limit, without repetition, there occurs that brilliant and rare thing which is called exuberance and which is equal to Beauty: "Exuberance is Beauty. The cistern contains, the fountain overflows." Amorous exuberance is the exuberance of the child whose narcissistic scope and multiple pleasure nothing (as yet) con-

Blake

BLAKE: *The Marriage of Heaven and Hell*, quoted by Norman O. Brown.

strains. Such exuberance can be interlaced with melancholy, with depressions and suicidal impulses, for the lover's discourse is not an *average* of states; but such a disequilibrium belongs to that black economy which marks me with its aberration and, so to speak, with its intolerable luxury.

The World Thunderstruck

déréalité / disreality

Sentiment of absence and withdrawal of reality
experienced by the amorous subject, confronting
the world.

1.   I. "I am waiting for a telephone call, and this
waiting makes me more anxious than usual. I try to do
something, but without much success. I walk back and
forth in my room: the various objects—whose familiarity
usually comforts me—the gray roofs, the noises of the
city, everything seems inert to me, cut off, thunder-
struck—like a waste planet, a Nature uninhabited by
man."

II. "I leaf through a book of reproductions of a painter I
love; I can do so only distractedly. I admire this work, but
the images are frozen, and this bores me."

III. "In a crowded restaurant, with friends, I am suffering
(an incomprehensible word for someone who is not in
love). This suffering comes to me from the crowd, from
the noise, from the decor (*kitsch*). A lid of disreality falls
over me from the lamps, the mirrored ceilings," etc.

IV. "I am alone in a café. It is Sunday, lunchtime. On the
other side of the glass, on a poster outside, Coluche
grimaces and plays the fool. I'm cold."

(The world is full without me, as in *Nausea;* the world plays at living behind a glass partition; the world is in an aquarium; I see everything close up and yet cut off, made of some other substance; I keep falling outside myself, without dizziness, without blur, into *precision.* as if I were drugged. "Oh, when this splendid Nature, spread out here before me, appears as frozen as a varnished miniature . . .")

2.   Any general conversation which I am obliged to listen to (if not to take part in) appalls me, paralyzes me. As for this language of the others from which I am excluded, it seems to me that these others overload it absurdly: they assert, object, argue, show off: what have I to do with Portugal, affection for dogs, or the latest *Petit Rapporteur?* I see the world—the other world—as a generalized hysteria.

3.   To escape disreality—to postpone its advent—I try to link myself to the world by bad temper. I *discourse* against something: "Landing in Rome, I see all Italy collapsing before my eyes; not a single item of merchandise attracts me in the shop windows; walking down the entire length of the Via dei Condotti, where ten years ago I had bought a silk shirt and thin summer socks, I find nothing but dime-store items. At the airport, the taxi driver wanted 14,000 lire instead of 7,000 because it was Corpus Christi. This country is losing on both counts: it is abolishing the differences in tastes, but not the division of classes," etc. Moreover, it suffices that I go on a little further for this aggressiveness, which keeps me lively, linked to the world, to turn to dereliction: I enter the dim

waters of disreality. "Piazza del Popolo (a holiday), with everyone talking, is showing off (isn't that what language is, showing off?), families, families, *maschi* strutting up and down, a grim and bustling populace," etc. I am *de trop* here, but—and this is a double grief—what I am excluded from is not desirable to me. Still, this way of speaking, by a last thread of language (that of the fine Sentence), keeps me on the brink of reality which withdraws and gradually freezes over, like young Werther's varnished miniature (Nature, today, is the City).

4.   I experience reality as a system of power. Coluche, the restaurant, the painter, Rome on a holiday, everything imposes on me its system of being; everyone is *badly behaved*. Isn't their impoliteness merely a *plenitude?* The world is full, plenitude is its system, and as a final offense this system is presented as a "nature" with which I must sustain good relations: in order to be "normal" (exempt from love), I should find Coluche funny, the restaurant J. good, T.'s painting beautiful, and the feast of Corpus Christi lively: not only undergo the system of power, but even enter into sympathy with it: "to love" reality? What disgust for the lover (for the lover's *virtue*)! It would be like Justine in the Monastery of Sainte-Marie-des-Bois.

Sade

So long as I perceive the world as hostile, I remain linked to it: *I am not crazy.* But sometimes, once my bad temper is exhausted, I have no language left at all: the world is not "unreal" (I could then utter it: there are arts of the unreal, among them the greatest arts of all), but disreal: reality has fled from it, is nowhere, so that I no longer have any meaning (any paradigm) available to me; *I do not manage* to define my relations with Coluche, the restaurant, the painter, the Piazza del Popolo. What relation can I have with a system of power if I am neither its slave nor its accomplice nor its witness?

5.   From my seat in the café, I see Coluche frozen there on the other side of the glass, laboriously preposterous. I find him to be idiotic to the second degree: idiotic to be playing the fool. My gaze is implacable, like a dead man's gaze; I laugh at no performance, however hilarious, I accept no wink of complicity; I am severed from any "associative traffic": on his poster, Coluche fails to make me associate: my conscience is cut in two by the café window.

Freud

6.   Sometimes the world is *unreal* (I utter it differently), sometimes it is *disreal* (I utter it with only the greatest difficulty if at all).

This is not (it is said) the same withdrawal from reality. In the first case, my rejection of reality is pronounced through a *fantasy:* everything around me changes value in relation to a function, which is the Image-repertoire; the lover then cuts himself off from the world, he unrealizes it because he hallucinates from another aspect the peripeteias or the utopias of his love; he surrenders himself to the Image, in relation to which all "reality" disturbs him. In the second case, I also lose reality, but no imaginary substitution will compensate me for this loss: sitting in front of the Coluche poster, I am not "dreaming" (even of the other); I am not even in the Image-repertoire any longer. Everything is frozen, petrified, immutable, i.e., *un-*

Lacan

FREUD: "Associative traffic," Freud apropos of hysteria and hypnosis—or Chertok apropos of hypnosis?
LACAN: *Le Séminaire,* I.

substitutable: the Image-repertoire is (temporarily) fore-closed. In the first moment I am neurotic, I unrealize; in the second, I am psychotic, crazy, I disrealize.

(Yet if I manage, by some mastery of writing, *to utter* this death, I begin to live again; I can posit antitheses, release exclamations, I can sing:

Verlaine
> *Qu'il était bleu, le ciel, et grand l'espoir!*
> *—L'espoir a fui, vaincu, vers le ciel noir . . .*
> How blue the sky was, and how great was hope!
> Hope has fled, conquered, to the black sky . . .)

7.   The unreal is uttered, abundantly (a thousand novels, a thousand poems). But the disreal cannot be uttered; for if I utter it (if I lunge at it, even with a clumsy or overliterary sentence), I emerge from it. Here I am in the buffet of the Lausanne railway station; at the next table, two Swiss are chattering; all of a sudden comes, for me, a free fall into the hole of disreality; but I can very quickly give this fall its insignia; that's what it is, I tell myself: "a ponderous stereotype spoken by a Swiss voice in the buffet of the Lausanne railway station." Instead of this hole, a vivid reality has just appeared: the reality of the Sentence (a madman who writes is never entirely mad; he is a *faker:* no Praise of Folly is possible).

8.   Sometimes, in a flash, I wake up and reverse the direction of my fall. After I have waited anxiously in my room in some unknown huge hotel in a foreign country, far away from my habitual little world, suddenly a power-ful sentence surfaces within my consciousness: *"But what*

VERLAINE: *"Colloque sentimental," Les Fêtes galantes.*

the hell am I doing here?" It is love which then appears to
be *disreal*.

Lautréamont

(Where are "things"? In amorous space, or in mundane
space? Where is "the childish underside of things"? What
is it which is childish? Is it "singing the boredom, the
suffering, the sadness, the darkness and death," etc.—
which it is said the lover does? Or is it, on the contrary:
speaking, gossiping, chattering, picking over the world and
its violence, its conflicts, its stakes, its *generality*—which
is what the others do?)

Novel/Drama

drame / drama

The amorous subject cannot write his love story himself. Only a very archaic form can accommodate the event which he declaims without being able to recount.

1.　In the letters he sends to his friend, Werther recounts both the events of his life and the effects of his passion; but it is literature which governs this mixture. For if I keep a journal, we may doubt that this journal relates, strictly speaking, to *events*. The events of amorous life are so trivial that they gain access to writing only by an immense effort: one grows discouraged writing what, *by being written,* exposes its own platitude: "I ran into X, who was with Y" "Today X didn't call me" "X was in a bad mood," etc.: who would see a story in that? The infinitesimal event exists only in its huge reverberation: *Journal of my reverberations* (of my wounds, my joys, my interpretations, my rationalizations, my impulses): who would understand anything in that? Only the Other could write my love story, my novel.

2.　As Narrative (Novel, Passion), love is a story which is accomplished, in the sacred sense of the word: it is a *program* which must be completed. For me, on the contrary, this story has *already taken place;* for what is event is exclusively the delight of which I have been the object and whose aftereffects I repeat (and fail to

Nietzsche

achieve). Enamoration is a *drama,* if we restore to this word the archaic meaning Nietzsche gives it: "Ancient drama envisioned great declamatory scenes, which excluded action (action took place *before* or *behind* the stage)." Amorous seduction (a pure hypnotic moment) takes place *before* discourse and *behind* the proscenium of consciousness: the amorous "event" is of a hieratic order: it is my own local legend, my little sacred history that I declaim to myself, and this declamation of a *fait accompli* (frozen, embalmed, removed from any *praxis*) is the lover's discourse.

NIETZSCHE: *The Case of Wagner.*

Flayed

écorché / flayed

The particular sensibility of the amorous subject,
which renders him vulnerable, defenseless to
the slightest injuries.

Freud

1.   I am "a mass of irritable substance." I have no
skin (except for caresses). Parodying Socrates in the
Phaedrus, one should speak of the Flayed Man, and not
the Feathered Man, in matters of love.

The resistance of the wood varies depending on the place
where we drive in the nail: wood is not isotropic. Nor am
I; I have my "exquisite points." The map of these points is
known to me alone, and it is according to them that I
make my way, avoiding or seeking this or that, depending
on externally enigmatic counsel; I should like this map of
moral acupuncture to be distributed preventively to my

R.H.

new acquaintances (who, moreover, could *also* utilize it to
make me suffer more).

2.   In order to find the grain of the wood (if one is not
a cabinetmaker), one need merely drive in a nail and see
if it penetrates readily. In order to discover my exquisite
points, there exists an instrument which resembles a nail:
this instrument is a joke: I do not suffer jokes lightly. The
Image-repertoire is, in fact, a serious matter (nothing to
do with being "serious-minded": the lover is not a man of

R.H.: Conversation.

good conscience): the child who is off in the moon (the *lunar* child) is not a playful child; I, in the same way, am cut off from playing: not only does play continuously risk bruising one of my exquisite points, but even everything the world finds amusing seems sinister to me; you cannot tease me without danger: irritable, hypersensitive? —Let us say, rather, tender, easily crushed, like the fiber of certain kinds of wood.

(The subject who is under the ascendancy of the Image-repertoire "offers" nothing in the play of the signifier: he dreams little, never pens. If he writes, his writing is smooth as an Image, always seeking to reinstate a legible surface of the words: anachronistic, in short, with regard to the modern text—which, *a contrario,* is defined by the abolition of the Image-repertoire: nothing "novelistic," no simulated Image: for Imitation, Representation, and Analogy are forms of coalescence: outmoded.)

Inexpressible Love

écrire / to write

Enticements, arguments, and impasses generated
by the desire to "express" amorous feeling in a
"creation" (particularly of writing).

Symposium

1.   Two powerful myths have persuaded us that love
could, *should* be sublimated in aesthetic creation: the
Socratic myth (loving serves to "engender a host of beautiful discourses") and the romantic myth (I shall produce
an immortal work by writing my passion).

Werther

Yet Werther, who used to draw abundantly and skillfully,
cannot draw Charlotte's portrait (he can scarcely sketch
her silhouette, which is precisely the thing about her that
first captivated him). "I have lost . . . the sacred, life-
giving power with which I created worlds about me."

2.

haiku

> The full moon this fall,
> All night long
> I have paced around the pond.

No indirect means could be more effective in the expression of sadness than that "all night long." What if I were
to try it, myself?

> This summer morning, the bay sparkling,
> I went outside
> To pick a wistaria.

or:

> This morning, the bay sparkling,
> I stayed here, motionless,
> Thinking of who is gone.

On the one hand, this is saying nothing; on the other, it is saying too much: impossible to *adjust*. My expressive needs oscillate between the mild little haiku summarizing a huge situation, and a great flood of banalities. I am both too big and too weak for writing: I am *alongside it,* for writing is always dense, violent, indifferent to the infantile ego which solicits it. Love has of course a complicity with my language (which maintains it), but it cannot be *lodged* in my writing.

3.　　　I cannot *write myself*. What, after all, is this "I" who would write himself? Even as he would enter into the writing, the writing would take the wind out of his sails, would render him null and void—futile; a gradual dilapidation would occur, in which the other's image, too, would be gradually involved (to write *on* something is to outmode it), a disgust whose conclusion could only be: *what's the use?* What obstructs amorous writing is the illusion of expressivity: as a writer, or assuming myself to be one, I continue to fool myself as to the *effects* of language: I do not know that the word "suffering" expresses no suffering and that, consequently, to use it is not only to communicate nothing but even, and immediately, to annoy, to irritate (not to mention the absurdity). Someone would have to teach me that one cannot write without burying "sincerity" (always the Orpheus myth: not to turn back). What writing demands, and what any lover cannot grant it without laceration, is to sacrifice *a little* of his Image-repertoire, and to assure thereby, through his language, the assumption of a little reality. All I might produce, at best, is a writing of the Image-repertoire; and for

François
Wahl

FRANÇOIS WAHL: "No one rises to 'his' language without sacrificing to it a little of his image-repertoire, and it is because of this that something in language is committed to function within reality" (*"Chute"*).

that I would have to renounce the Image-repertoire of writing—would have to let myself be subjugated by my language, submit to the injustices (the insults) it will not fail to inflict upon the double Image of the lover and of his other.

Boehme

The language of the Image-repertoire would be precisely the utopia of language; an entirely original, paradisiac language, the language of Adam—"natural, free of distortion or illusion, limpid mirror of our senses, a sensual language (*die sensualische Sprache*)": "In the sensual language, all minds converse together, they need no other language, for this is the language of nature."

4. To try to write love is to confront the *muck* of language: that region of hysteria where language is both *too much* and *too little,* excessive (by the limitless expansion of the *ego,* by emotive submersion) and impoverished (by the codes on which love diminishes and levels it). Faced with the death of his baby son, in order to write (if only scraps of writing), Mallarmé submits himself to parental division:

Boucourechliev

> *Mère, pleure*
> *Moi, je pense.*
> Mother, weep
> While I think.

But the amorous relation has made me into an atopical subject—undivided: I am my own child: I am both mother and father (of myself, of the other): how would I divide the labor?

JAKOB BOEHME: Quoted by Norman O. Brown.
BOUCOURECHLIEV: *Thrène,* on a text by Mallarmé (*Tombeau pour Anatole,* edited by J.-P. Richard).

5.   To know that one does not write for the other, to know that these things I am going to write will never cause me to be loved by the one I love (the other), to know that writing compensates for nothing, sublimates nothing, that it is precisely *there where you are not*—this is the beginning of writing.

The Ghost Ship

errance / errantry

Though each love is experienced as unique and
though the subject rejects the notion of repeating it
elsewhere later on, he sometimes discovers in
himself a kind of diffusion of amorous desire; he
then realizes he is doomed to wander until he dies,
from love to love.

1.   How does a love end? —Then it does end? To tell
the truth, no one—except for the others—ever knows anything about it; a kind of innocence conceals the end of this
thing conceived, asserted, *lived* according to eternity.
Whatever the loved being becomes, whether he vanishes
or moves into the realm of Friendship, in any case I never
see him disappear: the love which is over and done with
passes into another world like a ship into space, lights no
longer winking: the loved being once echoed loudly, now
that being is entirely without resonance (the other never
disappears when and how we expect). This phenomenon
results from a constraint in the lover's discourse: I myself
cannot (as an enamored subject) construct my love story
to the end: I am its poet (its bard) only for the beginning;
the end, like my own death, belongs to others; it is up to
them to write the fiction, the external, mythic narrative.

2.   I always behave—I insist upon behaving, whatever
I am told and whatever my own discouragements may be,
as if love might someday be fulfilled, as if the Sovereign
Good were possible. Whence that odd dialectic which

causes one absolute love to succeed another without the least embarrassment, as if, by love, I acceded to another logic (the absolute is no longer obliged to be unique), to another temporality (from love to love, I live my vertical moments), to another music (this sound, without memory, severed from any construction, oblivious of what precedes it and of what follows, is in itself musical). I search, I begin, I try, I venture further, I run ahead, but I never know that I am ending: it is never said of the Phoenix that it dies, but only that it is reborn (then I can be reborn without dying?).

Werther

Once I am not fulfilled and yet *do not kill myself,* amorous errantry is a fatality. Werther himself experienced it—shifting from "poor Leonora" to Charlotte; the impulse, of course, is checked; but if it had survived, Werther would have rewritten the same letters to another woman.

R.S.B.

Wagner

3.   Amorous errantry has its comical side: it resembles a ballet, more or less nimble according to the velocity of the fickle subject; but it is also a grand opera. The accursed Dutchman is doomed to wander the seas until he has found a woman who will be eternally faithful. I am that Flying Dutchman; I cannot stop wandering (loving) because of an ancient sign which dedicated me, in the remote days of my earliest childhood, to the god of my Image-repertoire, afflicting me with a compulsion to speak which leads me to say "I love you" in one port of call after another, until some other receives this phrase and gives it back to me; but no one can assume the impossible reply (of an insupportable fulfillment), and my wandering, my errantry continues.

R.S.B.: Conversation.

4.   Throughout life, all of love's "failures" resemble
one another (and with reason: they all proceed from the
same flaw). X and Y have not been able (have not
wanted) to answer my "demand," to adhere to my
"truth"; they have not altered their system one iota; for
me, the former has merely repeated the latter. And yet X
and Y are incomparable; it is in their difference, the model
of an infinitely pursued difference, that I find the energy to
begin all over again. The "perpetual mutability" (*in in-
constantia constans*) which animates me, far from
squeezing all those I encounter into the same functional
type (not to answer my demand), violently dislocates
their false community: errantry does not align—it produces iridescence: what results is the nuance. Thus I move
on, to the end of the tapestry, from one nuance to the next
(the nuance is the last state of a color which can be
named; the nuance is the Intractable).

"In the loving calm of your arms"

étreinte / embrace

The gesture of the amorous embrace seems to
fulfill, for a time, the subject's dream of total
union with the loved being.

Duparc

1.   Besides intercourse (when the Image-repertoire
goes to the devil), there is that other embrace, which is a
motionless cradling: we are enchanted, bewitched: we are
in the realm of sleep, without sleeping; we are within the
voluptuous infantilism of *sleepiness:* this is the moment
for telling stories, the moment of the voice which takes
me, siderates me, this is the return to the mother ("In the
loving calm of your arms," says a poem set to music by
Duparc). In this companionable incest, everything is suspended: time, law, prohibition: nothing is exhausted,
nothing is wanted: all desires are abolished, for they seem
definitively fulfilled.

2.   Yet, within this infantile embrace, the genital unfailingly appears; it cuts off the diffuse sensuality of the
incestuous embrace; the logic of desire begins to function,
the will-to-possess returns, the adult is superimposed upon
the child. I am then two subjects at once: I want maternity

DUPARC: *"Chanson triste,"* poem by Jean Lahor. Second-rate poetry?
But "second-rate poetry" takes the amorous subject into the linguistic
register which is all his own: *expression.*

and genitality. (The lover might be defined as a child getting an erection: such was the young Eros.)

3.　　A moment of affirmation; for a certain time, though a finite one, a *deranged* interval, something has been successful: I have been fulfilled (all my desires abolished by the plenitude of their satisfaction): fulfillment does exist, and I shall keep on making it return: through all the meanderings of my amorous history, I shall persist in wanting to rediscover, to renew the contradiction—the contraction—of the two embraces.

Exiled from the
Image-repertoire

Deciding to give up the amorous condition, the
subject sadly discovers himself exiled from his
Image-repertoire.

1.   Let me take Werther at that fictive moment (in the
fiction itself) when he might have renounced suicide. Then
the only thing left to him is exile: not to leave Charlotte
(he has already done so once, with no result), but to exile
himself from her image, or worse still: to cut off that
raving energy known as the Image-repertoire. Then begins
Hugo   "a kind of long insomnia." That is the price to be paid:
Freud   the death of the Image for my own life.

(Amorous passion is a delirium; but such delirium is not
alien; everyone speaks of it, it is henceforth tamed. What
is enigmatic is *the loss of delirium:* one returns to . . .
what?)

2.   In real mourning, it is the "test of reality" which
shows me that the loved object has ceased to exist. In
amorous mourning, the object is neither dead nor remote.
It is I who decide that its image must die (and I may go so

HUGO: "Exile is a kind of long insomnia" (*Pierres*).
FREUD: "Mourning incites the ego to renounce the object by declaring
that this latter is dead and by offering the ego the reward of remaining
alive."

far as to hide this death from it). As long as this strange mourning lasts, I will therefore have to undergo two contrary miseries: to suffer from the fact that the other is present (continuing, in spite of himself, to wound me) and to suffer from the fact that the other is dead (dead at least as I loved him). Thus I am wretched (an old habit) over a telephone call which does not come, but I must remind myself at the same time that this silence, *in any case,* is insignificant, since I have decided to get over any such concern: it was merely an aspect of the amorous image that it was to telephone me; once this image is gone, the telephone, whether it rings or not, resumes its trivial existence.

(Isn't the most sensitive point of this mourning the fact that I must *lose a language*—the amorous language? No more "I love you's.")

3.   Mourning for the image, insofar as I fail to perform it, makes me anxious; but insofar as I succeed in performing it, makes me sad. If exile from the Image-repertoire is the necessary road to "cure," it must be admitted that such progress is a sad one. This sadness is not a melancholy—or, at least, it is an incomplete melancholy (and not at all a clinical one), for I accuse myself of nothing, nor am I prostrated. My sadness belongs to that fringe of melancholy where the loss of the loved being remains abstract. A double lack: I cannot even invest my misery, as I could when I suffered from being in love. In those days I desired, dreamed, struggled; the benefit lay before me, merely delayed, traversed by contretemps.

Freud

FREUD: "In certain circumstances, we may observe that the l͟ . ᵃ less concrete nature. The object, for instance, is not actuall͟ only lost as an object of love . . ."

Now, no more resonance. Everything is calm, and that is worse. Though justified by an economy—the image dies so that I may live—amorous mourning always has something left over: one expression keeps recurring: "What a shame!"

4.   A proof of love: I sacrifice my Image-repertoire to you—the way a head of hair used to be dedicated. Thus, perhaps (at least, so it is said) I shall accede to "true love." If there is some resemblance between the amorous crisis and the analytic cure, I then go into mourning for my beloved, as the patient goes into mourning for his analyst: I liquidate my transference, and apparently this is how both the cure and the crisis end up. However, as has been pointed out, this theory forgets that the analyst, too, must go into mourning for his patient (or else the analysis risks being interminable); in the same way, the loved being—if I sacrifice to that being an Image-repertoire which nonetheless importuned him—the loved being must enter into the melancholy of his own collapse. And concurrently with my own mourning, I must anticipate and assume this melancholy on the part of the other, from which I shall suffer, *for I love the other still.*

The true act of mourning is not to suffer from the loss of the loved object; it is to discern one day, on the skin of the relationship, a certain tiny stain, appearing there as the symptom of a certain death: for the first time I am doing harm to the one I love, involuntarily, of course, but *without panic.*

5.   I try to wrest myself away from the amorous Image-repertoire: but the Image-repertoire burns under-

Antoine
Compagnon

ANTOINE COMPAGNON: *"L'Analyse orpheline."*

neath, like an incompletely extinguished peat fire; it catches again; what was renounced reappears; out of the hasty grave suddenly breaks a long cry.

(Jealousies, anxieties, possessions, discourses, appetites, signs, once again amorous desire was burning everywhere. It was as if I were trying to embrace one last time, hysterically, someone about to die—someone for whom I was about to die: I was performing a denial of separation.)

Freud

Winnicott

FREUD: "This rebellion is sometimes so intense that the subject may reach the point of rejecting reality and clinging to the lost object by means of a hallucinatory psychosis of desire."

WINNICOTT: "Just before this loss is experienced, we may discern in the child, in the excessive utilization of the transitional object, the denial of the fear that this object may lose its signification" (*Playing and Reality*).

The Orange

fâcheux / irksome

Sentiment of slight jealousy which overcomes the
amorous subject when he sees the loved being's
interest attracted or distracted by persons, objects,
or occupations which in his eyes function as so
many secondary rivals.

Werther

1. Werther: "The oranges I had set aside, the only
ones as yet to be found, produced an excellent effect,
though at each slice which she offered, for politeness's
sake, to an indiscreet neighbor, I felt my heart to be somehow pierced through." The world is full of indiscreet
neighbors with whom I must share the other. The world is
in fact just that: *an obligation to share*. The world (the
worldly) is my rival. I am continually disturbed by in-
truders: a vague connection, met by chance and who
forces his way into our company, sits down at our table;
neighbors in the restaurant whose vulgarity visibly fascinates the other, to the point where he is unaware if I am
speaking to him or not; even an object, a book for instance, in which the other is absorbed (I am jealous of the
book). Everything is irksome which briefly erases the dual
relation, which alters the complicity and relaxes the
intimacy: "You belong to me as well," the world says.

2. Charlotte shares her orange for politeness's sake,
or, one might say, out of kindness; but these are motives
which do not satisfy the lover: "It was scarcely worth my
while to set aside these oranges for her, since she gives

them to others," Werther probably tells himself. Any obedience to worldly procedures appears as a compromise on the part of the loved being, and this compromise alters that being's image. An insoluble contradiction: on the one hand, Charlotte must certainly be "kind," since she is a perfect object; but on the other hand, this kindness must not have the effect of abolishing the privilege which constitutes my very being. This contradiction eventuates in a vague resentment; my jealousy is indeterminate: it is addressed quite as much to the intruder as to the loved being who receives the intruder's demand without seeming to suffer from it: I am *vexed* with the others, with the other, with myself (from which a "scene" can be generated).

Fade-out

fading / fade-out

Painful ordeal in which the loved being appears
to withdraw from all contact, without such
enigmatic indifference even being directed against
the amorous subject or pronounced to the
advantage of anyone else, world or rival.

The TEXT of our MIND (VOICE) MAKES THE IMAGE AND ALSO

1.   In the text, the fade-out of voices is a good thing;
the voices of the narrative come, go, disappear, overlap;
we do not know who is speaking; the text speaks, that is
all: no more image, nothing but language. But the other is
not a text, the other is an image, single and coalescent; if
the voice is lost, it is the entire image which vanishes (love
is monologic, maniacal; the text is heterologic, perverse).
The other's fade-out, when it occurs, makes me anxious
because it seems without cause and without conclusion.
Like a kind of melancholy mirage, the other withdraws
into infinity and I wear myself out trying to get there.

(When this garment was at the height of fashion, an Amer-
ican firm advertised the washed-out blue of its jeans by
claiming: *"It fades and fades and fades."* The loved being,
in the same way, endlessly withdraws and pales: a feeling
of madness, purer than if this madness were violent.)

Proust

(Lacerating fade-out: just before dying, the Narrator's
grandmother, for moments at a time, neither sees nor
hears; she no longer recognizes the child, and stares at him
"with an astonished, suspicious, scandalized look.")

PROUST: *The Guermantes' Way.*

2.   There are nightmares in which the Mother appears, her face hardened into a cold and severe expression. The fade-out of the loved object is the terrifying return of the Wicked Mother, the inexplicable retreat of love, the well-known abandonment of which the Mystics complain: God exists, the Mother is present, but *they no longer love.* I am not destroyed, but *dropped here,* a reject.

3.   Jealousy causes less suffering, for at least the other remains vivid and alive. In the fade-out, the other seems to lose all desire, invaded by the Night. I am abandoned by the other, but this abandonment is intensified by the abandonment the other himself suffers; his image is thereby washed out, liquidated; I can no longer sustain myself upon anything, even the desire the other might experience elsewhere: I am in mourning for an object which is itself in mourning (which suggests how much we need the other's desire, even if this desire is not addressed to us).

John of the Cross

4.   When the other is affected by this fade-out, when he withdraws for no particular reason except an anxiety accounted for only in these wretched words: *"I don't feel well,"* he seems to move away in a mist; not dead, but *living without contour* in the realm of the Shades; Ulysses visited them, called them up, finding among them the shade of his mother; thus I appeal to and summon up the other, the Mother, but what comes is merely a shade.

JOHN OF THE CROSS: "We call *Night* the privation of relish in the appetite for all things."
ODYSSEY: Book XI.

5.　　The other's fade-out resides in his voice. The voice supports, evinces, and so to speak performs the disappearance of the loved being, for it is characteristic of the voice to die. What constitutes the voice is what, within it, lacerates me by dint of having to die, as if it were at once and never could be anything but a memory. This phantom being of the voice is what is dying out, it is that sonorous texture which disintegrates and disappears. I never know the loved being's voice except when it is dead, remembered, recalled inside my head, way past the ear; a tenuous yet monumental voice, since it is one of those objects which exist only once they have disappeared.

(A voice asleep, a voice no longer inhabited, a voice acknowledging, at a great distance, the blank fatality.)

6.　　Nothing more lacerating than a voice at once beloved and exhausted: a broken, rarefied, bloodless voice, one might say, a voice from the end of the world, which will be swallowed up far away by cold depths: such a voice is *about* to vanish, as the exhausted being is *about* to die: fatigue is infinity: what never manages to end. That brief, momentary voice, almost ungracious in its rarity, that *almost nothing* of the loved and distant voice, becomes in me a sort of monstrous cork, as if a surgeon were thrusting a huge plug of wadding into my head.

7.　　Freud, apparently, did not like the telephone, however much he may have liked *listening*. Perhaps he felt, perhaps he foresaw that the telephone is always a *cacophony*, and that what it transmits is the *wrong voice*,

MARTIN FREUD: *Sigmund Freud, Man and Father.*

Winnicott

the false communication . . . No doubt I try to deny separation by the telephone—as the child fearing to lose its mother keeps pulling on a string; but the telephone wire is not a good transitional object, it is not an inert string; it is charged with a meaning, which is not that of junction but that of distance: the loved, exhausted voice heard over the telephone is the fade-out in all its anxiety. First of all, this voice, when it reaches me, when it is here, while it (with great difficulty) survives, is a voice I never entirely recognize; as if it emerged from under a mask (thus we are told that the masks used in Greek tragedy had a magical function: to give the voice a chthonic origin, to distort, to alienate the voice, to make it come from somewhere under the earth). Then, too, on the telephone the other is always in a situation of departure; the other departs twice over, by voice and by silence: whose turn is it to speak? We fall silent in unison: crowding of two voids. *I'm going to leave you,* the voice on the telephone says with each second.

Proust

(Episode of anxiety experienced by the Proustian narrator, when he telephones his grandmother: anxiety conferred by the telephone: the true signature of love.)

8.   I am alarmed by everything which appears to alter the Image. I am, therefore, alarmed by the other's fatigue: it is the cruelest of all rival objects. How combat exhaustion? I can see that the other, exhausted, tears off a fragment of this fatigue *in order to give it to me.* But what am I to do with this bundle of fatigue set down before me?

WINNICOTT: "I explained to the mother that her son dreaded the separation he was attempting to deny by pulling on the string, just as we deny our separation from a friend by resorting to the telephone" (*Playing and Reality*).
PROUST: *The Guermantes' Way.*

What does this gift mean? *Leave me alone? Take care of me?* No one answers, for what is given is precisely *what does not answer.*

(In no love story I have ever read is a character ever *tired.* I had to wait for Blanchot for someone to tell me about Fatigue.)

Blanchot

BLANCHOT: Conversation (long ago).

At Fault

fautes / faults

In various contingencies of everyday life, the
subject imagines he has failed the loved being and
thereby experiences a sentiment of guilt.

1.   "As soon as they reached the train station, he
noticed, though without mentioning it, a signboard giving
the location of the second-class cars and of the dining car;
the locations seemed so far away, at the very end of the
curving platform, that he had not dared take the precaution—after all, an overprotective one—of leading X in
that direction to wait for the train; it would have been, he
thought, a kind of cowardice, an obsequious submission to
the railway code: studying signboards, terror of being late,
surrender to platform hysterics—were they not all char-
acteristics of the old, the infirm? Besides, suppose he was
mistaken? How silly to run all the way down the platform,
like those fools who limp along, loaded down with pack-
ages! Yet that is just what happened: the train passed
through the station and stopped very far down the track.
X gave him a quick hug and ran ahead; as did several
young vacationers in bathing suits. After that, he saw
nothing more, except the bulging rear end of the last car,
far ahead. No sign (such a thing was impossible), no
farewell. The train still did not move. Yet he dared not
move, leave the platform, though it was quite useless to
remain where he was. A kind of symbolic constraint (the
powerful constraint of a minor symbolism) forced him to
stay where he was, as long as the train stayed there (with
X inside). So he didn't move, stupid, seeing nothing ex-

cept the faraway train, seen by no one on the empty platform—impatient, finally, for the train to leave. But he
would have been at fault had he left first, and this fault
might have haunted him for a long time."

2. Any fissure within Devotion is a fault: that is the
rule of *Cortezia*. This fault occurs whenever I make any

cortezia

gesture of independence with regard to the loved object;
each time I attempt, in order to break my servitude, to
"think for myself" (the world's unanimous advice), I feel
guilty. What I am guilty of, then, is paradoxically lighten-
ing the burden, reducing the exorbitant load of my devotion—in short, "managing" (according to the world); in
fact, it is being strong which frightens me, it is control (or
its gesticulation) which makes me guilty.

3. Every pain, every misfortune, Nietzsche remarks,
has been falsified by a notion of guilt, of being at fault:

Nietzsche

"We have deprived pain of its innocence." Passionate love
(the lover's discourse) keeps succumbing to this falsifica-
tion. Yet there might be the possibility of an innocent
suffering in this kind of love, of an innocent misery (if I
were faithful to the pure Image-repertoire, and if I were to
reproduce within myself only the infantile dyad, the suffering of the child separated from its mother); I should then
not accuse what lacerates me, I might even *affirm* suffering. Such would be the innocence of passion: not a purity
at all, but quite simply the rejection of Fault. The lover
would be as innocent as Sade's heroes. Unfortunately, his
suffering is in most cases intensified by its double, Wrong-
doing: I am frightened by the other "more than by my

Symposium

father."

SYMPOSIUM: Phaedrus: "If a man in love commits some misdeed . . . he
will suffer much more at being observed in it by his love than by his
father."

"*Special Days*"

fête / festivity

The amorous subject experiences every meeting with the loved being as a festival.

1. The Festivity is what is waited for, what is expected. What I expect of the promised presence is an unheard-of totality of pleasures, a banquet; I rejoice like the child laughing at the sight of the mother whose mere presence heralds and signifies a plenitude of satisfactions: I am about to have before me, and for myself, the "source of all good things."

Lacan

Werther

"I am living through days as happy as those God keeps for his chosen people; and whatever becomes of me, I can never say that I have not tasted the purest joys of life."

2. "That night—I tremble to speak of it!—I held her in my arms, pressed to my heart, I kept kissing her lips, which murmured words of love, and my eyes drowned in the intoxication of hers! Lord God, am I to blame if even now I experience a heavenly joy in recalling those passionate pleasures, in reliving them in the depths of my being!"

Werther

For the Lover, the Man-in-the-Moon, the Festivity is a jubilation, not an explosion: I delight in the dinner, the conversation, the tenderness, the secure promise of pleasure: "an *ars vivendi* over the abyss."

ean-Louis Bouttes

(Then is it nothing, for you, to be someone's festivity?)

JEAN-LOUIS BOUTTES: *Le Destructeur d'intensité.*

"I am crazy"

fou / mad

It frequently occurs to the amorous subject that
he is or is going mad.

1.   I am mad to be in love, I am not mad to be able to
say so, I double my image: insane in my own eyes (I know
my delirium), simply unreasonable in the eyes of someone
else, to whom I quite sanely describe my madness: conscious of this madness, sustaining a discourse upon it.

Werther

Werther meets a madman in the mountains: in midwinter,
he wants to pick flowers for Charlotte, whom he has
loved. This man, during the time he was in a padded cell,
was happy: he no longer knew anything about himself.
Werther *half* recognizes himself in the madman seeking
flowers: mad with passion, like himself, but deprived of
any access to the (supposed) happiness of unconscious-
ness: he suffers from having failed his own madness.

2.   Every lover is mad, we are told. But can we
imagine a madman in love? Never—I am entitled only to
an impoverished, incomplete, *metaphorical* madness: love
drives me *nearly* mad, but I do not communicate with the
supernatural, there is nothing of the sacred within me; my
madness, a mere irrationality, is dim, even invisible; besides, it is entirely recuperated by the culture: it frightens
no one. (Yet it is in the amorous state that certain rational
subjects suddenly realize that madness is very close at
hand, quite possible: a madness in which love itself would
founder.)

3. For a hundred years, (literary) madness has been thought to consist in Rimbaud's *"Je est un autre"*: madness is an experience of depersonalization. For me as an amorous subject, it is quite the contrary: it is becoming a *subject,* being unable to keep myself from doing so, which drives me mad. *I am not someone else:* that is what I realize with horror.

(A Zen story: An old monk busies himself in the hottest weather drying mushrooms. "Why don't you let others do that?" "Another man is not myself, and I am not another. Another cannot experience my action. I must create my experience of drying mushrooms.")

I am indefectibly myself, and it is in this that I am mad: I am mad because *I consist.*

4. A man is mad if he is pure of all power. —But doesn't the lover experience any excitation of power? Subjection, though, is my business: subjected, seeking to subject the other, I experience in my fashion the will to power, the *libido dominandi:* do I not possess, like political systems, a strong, *articulated* discourse? Yet this is my singularity: my libido is entirely enclosed: I inhabit no other space but the amorous duel: not an atom outside, hence not an atom of gregarity: *I am crazy,* not because I am original (a crude ruse of conformity), but because I am severed from all sociality. If other men are always, to various degrees, the militants of something, I am the soldier of nothing, not even of my own madness: *I do not socialize* (as it is said of someone that he doesn't symbolize).

St. Augustine

ST. AUGUSTINE: *Libido sentiendi, libido sciendi, libido excellendi (dominandi)* (Quoted by Sainte-Beuve).

"*Looking embarrassed*"

gêne / embarrassment

A group scene in which the implicit nature of the amorous relation functions as a constraint and provokes a collective embarrassment which is not spoken.

Werther

1.   Werther is making a scene (just before his suicide) with Charlotte, but the scene is interrupted by Albert's arrival. No one speaks, and the three move about in the room, looking embarrassed; various trivial subjects of conversation are launched, all of which fall flat. The situation is charged. With what? With the fact that each person is perceived by the other two in his role (of husband, of lover, of stake), without its being possible to take account of this role in the conversation. What is heavy is the silent knowledge: I know that you know that I know: this is the general formula of embarrassment, a frozen, white modesty which takes the insignificance (of remarks) as its insignia. Paradox: the unspoken as the symptom . . . of the *conscious*.

2.   Accident happens to bring together several friends in this café: a whole bundle of affects. The situation is charged; though I am involved in it and even suffer from it, I experience it as a scene, a carefully drawn and well-composed tableau (something like a slightly perverse

Greuze); the situation is crammed with meanings, I read them, I follow them in their last articulations; I observe, I decipher, I enjoy a text bursting with legibility *for the reason that it does not speak*. I merely *see* what is spoken, as in a silent movie. There is generated in me (a contradiction in terms) a kind of *alert fascination:* I am nailed to the scene and yet very wide awake: my attention constitutes a part of what is being acted out, nothing is external to the scene, and yet I read it: there are no footlights—this is an extreme theater. Whence the awkwardness—or, for some perverse types, the pleasure.

Gradiva

Gradiva / Gradiva

This name, borrowed from Jensen's book analyzed
by Freud, designates the image of the loved being
insofar as that being agrees to enter to some
degree into the amorous subject's delirium in order
to help him escape from it.

1.   The hero of *Gradiva* is an excessive lover: he
hallucinates what others would merely evoke. The classi-
cal Gradiva, a figure of the woman he loves unknowingly,
is perceived as a real person: that is his delirium. The
woman, in order to release him from it gently, initially
conforms to his delirium; she enters into it a little, con-
sents to play the part of Gradiva, to sustain the illusion
somewhat and not to waken the dreamer too abruptly,
gradually to unite myth and reality, by means of which the
Freud   amorous experience assumes something of the same function as an analytic cure.

2.   Gradiva is a figure of salvation, of fortunate
escape, a kindly Eumenid. But just as the Eumenides are
merely former Erinyes, goddesses of torment, there also
exists, in the amorous realm, a "wicked" Gradiva. The
loved being, if only unconsciously and for motives which
may proceed from his own neurotic advantage, then seems
to be determined to lodge me even deeper in my delirium,
to sustain and to aggravate the amorous wound: like those

FREUD: "We must not underestimate the curative power of love in
delirium" (*Delirium and Dream in Jensen's "Gradiva"*).

parents of schizophrenics who, it is said, continually provoke or aggravate their child's madness by minor conflictive interventions, the other attempts *to drive me mad*. For instance: the other sets about making me contradict myself (which has the effect of paralyzing any language in me); or again, the other alternates actions of seduction with actions of frustration (this is a commonplace of the amorous relation); the other shifts without warning from one regime to another, from intimate tenderness and complicity to coldness, to silence, to dismissiveness; or finally, in an even more tenuous fashion, though no less wounding, the other sets about "breaking" the conversation, either by forcing it to shift suddenly from a serious subject (which matters to me) to a trivial one, or by being obviously interested, while I am speaking, in something else than what I am saying. In short, the other keeps bringing me back to my own impasse: I can neither escape from this impasse nor rest within it, like the famous Cardinal Balue shut up in a cage where he could neither stand nor lie down.

3.   How can the being who has captured me, taken me in the net, release me, part the meshes? By delicacy. When Martin Freud, as a child, had been humiliated during a skating party, his father hears him out, speaks to him, and releases him, as if he were freeing an animal caught in a poacher's net: "Very tenderly, he parted the meshes which held the little creature, showing no haste and resisting without impatience the jerks the animal made to free itself, until he had disentangled them all and the creature could run away, forgetting all about the whole episode."

Freud

‣FREUD: Martin Freud: *Sigmund Freud, Man and Father*.

4.   It will be said to the lover—or to Freud: it was easy for the false Gradiva to enter somewhat into her lover's delirium, she loved him too. Or rather, explain to us this contradiction: on the one hand, Zoé wants Norbert (she wants to be one with him), she is in love with him; and on the other hand—an exorbitant thing for an amorous subject—she retains control over her feelings, she is not delirious, since she is capable of feigning. How then can Zoé both "love" and "be in love"? Are not these two projects supposed to be different, the one noble, the other morbid?

Loving and *being in love* have difficult relationships with each other: for if it is true that *being in love* is unlike anything else (a drop of *being-in-love* diluted in some vague friendly relation dyes it brightly, makes it incomparable: I know *right away* that in my relation with X, Y, however prudently I restrain myself, there is a certain amount of *being-in-love*), it is also true that in *being-in-love* there is a certain amount of *loving:* I want to possess, fiercely, but I also know how to give, actively. Then who can manage this dialectic successfully? Who, if not the F.W.   woman, the one who does not make for any object but only for . . . giving? So that if a lover manages to "love," it is precisely insofar as he feminizes himself, joins Winnicott   the class of *Grandes Amoureuses,* of Women Who Love Enough to Be Kind. Perhaps this is why it is Norbert who is delirious and Zoé who loves.

F.W.: Conversation.

Blue Coat and Yellow Vest

habit / habiliment

Any affect provoked or sustained by the clothing
which the subject has worn during the amorous
encounter, or wears with the intention of seducing
the loved object.

1.   Because of a forthcoming encounter—one I anticipate with exaltation—I dress very carefully, I perform
my toilet with every scruple. This word has only "official"
meanings; not to mention the scatological usage, it also
designates "the preparations given to the prisoner condemned to death before he is led to the scaffold"; or again,
"the transparent and oily membrane used by butchers to
cover certain cuts of meat." As if, at the end of every
toilet, inscribed within the excitation it provokes, there
were always the slaughtered, embalmed, varnished body,
prettified in the manner of a victim. In dressing myself, I
embellish that which, by desire, will be spoiled.

Littré

2.   Socrates: "I therefore have decked myself out in
finery so that I might be in the company of a fine young
man." I must resemble whom I love. I postulate (and it is
this which brings about my pleasure) a conformity of essence between the other and myself. Image, imitation: I
do as many things as I can in the other's fashion. I want to
be the other, I want the other to be me, as if we were

Symposium

united, enclosed within the same sack of skin, the garment being merely the smooth envelope of that coalescent substance out of which my amorous Image-repertoire is made.

3.   Werther: "How much it cost me to make myself give up the very simple blue coat that I was wearing the first time I danced with Lotte; but it had finally worn out altogether. So I had had another one made, absolutely identical to the first . . ." It is in this garment (blue coat and yellow vest) that Werther wants to be buried, and which he is wearing when he is found dying in his room. Each time he wears this garment (in which he will die), Werther disguises himself. As what? As an enchanted lover: he magically re-creates the episode of the enchantment, that moment when he was first transfixed by the Image. This blue garment imprisons him so effectively that the world around him vanishes: *nothing but the two of us:* by this garment, Werther forms for himself a child's body in which phallus and mother are united, with nothing left over. This perverse outfit was worn across Europe by the novel's enthusiasts, and it was known as a "costume à la Werther."

Werther

Lacan

Identifications

The subject painfully identifies himself with some person (or character) who occupies the same position as himself in the amorous structure.

1.   Werther identifies himself with every lost lover: he is the madman who loved Charlotte and goes out picking flowers in midwinter; he is the young footman in love with a widow, who has just killed his rival—indeed, Werther wants to intercede for this youth, whom he cannot rescue from the law: "Nothing can save you, poor wretch! Indeed, I see that nothing can save us." Identification is not a psychological process; it is a pure structural operation: I am the one who has the same place I have.

Werther

2.   I devour every amorous system with my gaze and in it discern the place which would be mine if I were a part of that system. I perceive not analogies but homologies: I note, for instance, that I am to X what Y is to Z; everything I am told about Y affects me powerfully, though Y's person is a matter of indifference to me, or even unknown; I am caught in a mirror which changes position and which reflects me wherever there is a dual structure. Worse still: it can happen that on the other hand I am loved by someone I do not love; now, far from helping me (by the gratification it implies or the diversion it might constitute), this situation is painful to me: I see myself in the other who loves without being loved, I rec-

ognize in him the very gestures of my own unhappiness, but this time it is I myself who am the active agent of this unhappiness: I experience myself both as victim and as executioner.

(It is because of this homology that the love story "works"—sells.)

3.   X is more or less desired, flattered, by others than by me. Hence I put myself in their place, as Werther is in the same place as Heinrich, the madman with the flowers, who has loved Charlotte to the point of madness. Now, this structural analogy (certain points are arranged in a certain order around one point) is readily imaginable in terms of personality: since Heinrich and I occupy the same place, it is no longer merely with Heinrich's place that I identify myself, but with his image as well. A hallucination seizes me: *I am Heinrich!* This generalized identification, extended to all those who surround the other and benefit from the other as I do, is doubly painful to me: it devalues me in my own eyes (I find myself *reduced* to a certain personality), but it also devalues my other, who becomes the inert object of a circle of rivals. Each, identical with the others, seems to be shouting: *Mine! mine!* Like a mob of children arguing over a ball or any other object; in short, over the fetish thrown into their midst.

Werther

The structure has nothing to do with persons; hence (like a bureaucracy) it is terrible. It cannot be implored—I cannot say to it: "Look how much better I am than H." Inexorable, the structure replies: "You are in the same place; hence you are H." No one can *plead* against the structure.

4.   Werther identifies himself with the madman, with
Werther   the footman. As a reader, I can identify myself with
Werther. Historically, thousands of subjects have done so,
suffering, killing themselves, dressing, perfuming themselves, writing as if they were Werther (songs, poems,
candy boxes, belt buckles, fans, colognes à la Werther). A
long chain of equivalences links all the lovers in the world.
In the theory of literature, "projection" (of the reader into
the character) no longer has any currency: yet it is the
appropriate tonality of imaginative readings: reading a
love story, it is scarcely adequate to say I project myself; I
cling to the image of the lover, shut up with this image in
the very enclosure of the book (everyone knows that such
stories are read in a state of secession, of retirement, of
Proust   voluptuous absence: in the toilet).

PROUST: (The orris-scented toilet, in Combray) "Intended for a more
particular and more vulgar purpose, this room . . . long served as a
refuge for me, doubtless because it was the only one where I was
allowed to lock the door, a refuge for all my occupations which required
an invincible solitude: reading, daydreaming, tears, and pleasure."

Images

In the amorous realm, the most painful wounds
are inflicted more often by what one sees than by
what one knows.

1.   ("Suddenly, coming back from the coatroom, he
sees them in intimate conversation, leaning close to one
another.")

The image is presented, pure and distinct as a letter: it is
the letter of what pains me. Precise, complete, definitive, it
leaves no room for me, down to the last finicky detail: I
am excluded from it as from the primal scene, which may
exist only insofar as it is framed within the contour of the
keyhole. Here then, at last, is the definition of the image,
of any image: that from which I am excluded. Contrary to
those puzzle drawings in which the hunter is secretly
figured in the confusion of the foliage, I am not in the
scene: the image is without a riddle.

2.   The image is peremptory, it always has the last
word; no knowledge can contradict it, "arrange" it, refine
it. Werther knows perfectly well that Charlotte is be-
trothed to Albert, and in fact only suffers vaguely from the
fact; but "his whole body shudders when Albert embraces
her slender waist." *I know perfectly well* that Charlotte
does not belong to me, says Werther's reason, *but all the*

Werther

same, Albert is stealing her from me, says the image which is before his eyes.

3.   The images from which I am excluded are cruel, yet sometimes I am caught up in the image (reversal). Leaving the outdoor café where I must *leave behind* the other with friends, *I see myself* walking away alone, shoulders bowed, down the empty street. I convert my exclusion into an image. This image, in which my absence is reflected as in a mirror, is a *sad* image.

Caspar David
Friedrich

A romantic painting shows a heap of icy debris in a polar light; no man, no object inhabits this desolate space; but for this very reason, provided I am suffering an amorous sadness, this void requires that I fling myself into it; I project myself there as a tiny figure, seated on a block of ice, abandoned forever. "I'm cold," the lover says, "let's go back"; but there is no road, no way, the boat is wrecked. There is a *coldness* particular to the lover, the chilliness of the child (or of any young animal) that needs maternal warmth.

4.   What wounds me are the *forms* of the relation, its images; or rather, what others call *form* I experience as force. The image—as the example for the obsessive—is *the thing itself.* The lover is thus an artist; and his world is in fact a world reversed, since in it each image is its own end (nothing beyond the image).

FRIEDRICH: *The Wreck of the "Hope."*

The Unknowable

inconnaissable / unknowable

Efforts of the amorous subject to understand and
define the loved being "in itself," by some
standard of character type, psychological or
neurotic personality, independent of the particular
data of the amorous relation.

1.   I am caught in this contradiction: on the one
hand, I believe I know the other better than anyone and
triumphantly assert my knowledge to the other ("*I* know
you—I'm the only one who really knows you!"); and on
the other hand, I am often struck by the obvious fact that
the other is impenetrable, intractable, not to be found; I
cannot open up the other, trace back the other's origins,
solve the riddle. Where does the other come from? Who is
the other? I wear myself out, I shall never know.

(Of everyone I had known, X was certainly the most
impenetrable. This was because you never knew anything
about his desire: isn't *knowing someone* precisely that—
knowing his desire? I knew everything, immediately, about
Y's desires, hence Y himself was obvious to me, and I was
inclined to love him no longer in a state of terror but
indulgently, the way a mother loves her child.)

Reversal: "I can't get to know you" means "I shall never
know what you really think of me." I cannot decipher you
because I do not know how you decipher me.

2.　　To expend oneself, to bestir oneself for an impenetrable object is pure religion. To make the other into an insoluble riddle on which my life depends is to consecrate the other as a god; I shall never manage to solve the question the other asks me, the lover is not Oedipus. Then all that is left for me to do is to reverse my ignorance into truth. It is not true that the more you love, the better you understand; all that the action of love obtains from me is merely this wisdom: that the other is not to be known; his opacity is not the screen around a secret, but, instead, a kind of evidence in which the game of reality and appearance is done away with. I am then seized with that exaltation of loving *someone unknown,* someone who will remain so forever: a mystic impulse: I know what I do not know.

Gide

3.　　Or again, instead of trying to define the other ("What is he?"), I turn to myself: "What do I want, wanting to know you?" What would happen if I decided to define you as a force and not as a person? And if I were to situate myself as another force confronting yours? This would happen: my other would be defined solely by the suffering or the pleasure he affords me.

GIDE: Speaking of his wife: "And since it always requires love in order to understand what differs from you . . ." (*Et nunc manet in te*).

"Show me whom to desire"

induction / induction

The loved being is desired because another or others have shown the subject that such a being is desirable: however particular, amorous desire is discovered by induction.

Werther

1. Shortly before falling in love, Werther meets a young footman who tells him of his passion for a widow: "The image of that fidelity, that tenderness, pursues me everywhere, and as though scorched myself by that fire, I faint, I fail, consuming myself." After which there is nothing left for Werther to do but to fall in love in his turn, with Charlotte. And Charlotte herself will be pointed out to him, before he sees her; in the carriage taking them to the ball, an obliging friend tells him how lovely she is. The body *which will be loved* is in advance selected and manipulated by the lens, subjected to a kind of zoom effect which magnifies it, brings it closer, and leads the subject to press his nose to the glass: is it not the *scintillating* object which a skillful hand causes to shimmer before me and

Freud

which will hypnotize me, capture me? This "affective contagion," this induction, proceeds from others, from the language, from books, from friends: no love is original.

La Rochefoucauld

(Mass culture is a machine for showing desire: here is

LA ROCHEFOUCAULD: "Some people would never have been in love, had they never heard love talked about."

Stendhal

what must interest you, it says, as if it guessed that men are incapable of finding what to desire by themselves.)

The difficulty of the amorous project is in this: "Just show me whom to desire, but then get out of the way!": Countless episodes in which I fall in love with someone loved by my best friend: every rival has first been a master, a guide, a barker, a mediator.

2.   In order to show you where your desire is, it is enough to forbid it to you *a little* (if it is true that there is no desire without prohibition). X wants me to be there, beside him, while leaving him free *a little:* flexible, going away occasionally, but *not far:* on the one hand, I must be present as a prohibition (without which there would not be the right desire), but also I must go away the moment when, this desire having formed, I might be in its way: I

Winnicott

must be the Mother who loves enough (protective and generous), around whom the child plays, while she peacefully knits or sews. This would be the structure of the "successful" couple: a little prohibition, a good deal of play; to designate desire and then to leave it alone, like those obliging natives who show you the path but don't insist on accompanying you on your way.

STENDHAL: "Before love is born, beauty is necessary as a sign, it predisposes to this passion by the praises we hear bestowed upon whom we will love" (*On Love*).

The Informer

informateur / informer

A friendly figure whose constant role, however,
seems to be to wound the amorous subject by
"innocently" furnishing commonplace information
about the loved being, though the effect of this
information is to disturb the subject's image of
that being.

1. Gustave, Léon, and Richard form a group;
Urbain, Claudius, Etienne, and Ursule, another; Abel,
Gontran, Angèle, and Hubert, still another (I borrow these
names from *Paludes,* which is the book of First Names).
However, Léon happens to meet Urbain, who gets to
know Angèle, who knew Léon slightly anyway, etc. Thus
is formed a constellation; each subject is called upon to
enter into relations, one day or another, with the star re-
motest from him and to become involved with that particular star out of all the rest: everything ends by coinciding
(this is the precise impulse of *A la recherche du temps
perdu,* which is, among other things, a tremendous in-
trigue, a farce network). Worldly friendship is epidemic:
everyone catches it, like a disease. Now suppose that I
release into this network a suffering subject eager to main-
tain with his other a pure, sealed space (consecrated, un-
touched); the network's activities, its exchange of information, its interests and initiatives will be received as so
many dangers. And in the center of this little society, at
once an ethnological village and a boulevard comedy,
parental structure and comic imbroglio, stands the Informer, who busies himself and *tells everyone everything.*

Gide

Proust

Ingenuous or perverse, the Informer has a negative role.
However anodyne the message he gives me (like a disease), he reduces my other to being merely another. I am
of course obliged to listen to him (I cannot *in worldly
terms* allow my vexation to be seen), but I strive to make
my listening flat, indifferent, impervious.

2.   What I want is a little cosmos (with its own time,
its own logic) inhabited only by "the two of us." Everything from outside is a threat; either in the form of boredom (if I must live in a world from which the other is
absent), or in the form of injury (if that world supplies
me with an indiscreet discourse concerning the other).
By furnishing me insignificant information about the one I
love, the Informer discovers a secret for me. This secret is
not a deep one, but comes from outside: it is the other's
"outside" which was hidden from me. The curtain rises
the wrong way round—not on an intimate stage, but on
the crowded theater. Whatever it tells me, the information
is painful: a dull, ungrateful fragment of reality lands on
me. For the lover's delicacy, every fact has something
aggressive about it: a bit of "science," however commonplace, invades the Image-repertoire.

Buñuel

BUÑUEL: *The Discreet Charm of the Bourgeoisie.*

This can't go on

insupportable / unbearable

The sentiment of an accumulation of amorous
sufferings explodes in this cry: "This can't
go on . . ."

1.   At the novel's end, with a phrase which will pre-
cipitate Werther's suicide, Charlotte (who has her problems, too) finally remarks that "things cannot go on like
this." Werther might have said as much himself, and quite
early in the book, for it is proper to the amorous situation
to be immediately intolerable, once the magical amaze-
ment of the first encounter is past. A demon denies time,
change, growth, dialectic, and says at every moment: *This
can't go on!* Yet it goes on, it lasts, if not forever, at least
a long time. Thus amorous patience has as its motor its
own denial: it proceeds neither from a kind of waiting, an
expectation, nor from mastery or ruse, nor from courage:
it is an unhappiness which does not wear itself out in
proportion to its acuity; a succession of jolts, the
(comic?) repetition of the gesture by which I signify to
myself that I have—courageously!—decided to put an end
to the repetition; the patience of an impatience.
(*Reasonable* sentiment: everything works out, but nothing
lasts. *Amorous* sentiment: nothing works out, but it keeps
going on.)

2.   To acknowledge the Unbearable: this cry has its
advantage: signifying to myself that I must escape by

whatever means, I establish within myself the martial theater of Decision, of Action, of Outcome. *Exaltation* is a kind of secondary profit from my impatience; I feed on it, I wallow in it. Ever the "artist," I make form itself into content. Imagining a painful outcome (renouncing, leaving, etc.), I intone, within myself, the exalted hallucination of closure; a vainglory of abnegation seizes me (renouncing love but not friendship, etc.), and I immediately forget what I would then have to sacrifice: my madness itself—which by its very status cannot be constituted as the object of my sacrifice: who ever saw a madman "sacrificing" his madness to someone? For the moment, I regard abnegation as only a noble, theatrical form; in other words, I still keep it within the enclosure of my Image-repertoire.

3.   Once the exaltation has lapsed, I am reduced to the simplest philosophy: that of endurance (the natural dimension of real fatigues). I suffer without adjustment, I persist without intensity: always bewildered, never discouraged; I am a Daruma doll, a legless toy endlessly poked and pushed, but *finally* regaining its balance, assured by an inner balancing pin (But what is my balancing pin? The *force* of love?). This is what we are told by a folk poem which accompanies these Japanese dolls:

> Such is life
> Falling over seven times
> And getting up eight.

Ideas of Solution

issues / outcomes

Enticement of solutions, whatever they may be,
which afford the amorous subject, despite their
frequently catastrophic character, a temporary
peace; hallucinatory manipulation of the possible
outcomes of the amorous crisis.

1.　　Idea of suicide; idea of separation; idea of withdrawal; idea of travel; idea of sacrifice, etc.; I can imagine
several solutions to the amorous crisis, and I keep doing
so. Yet, however alienated I may be, it is not difficult for
me to grasp, through all these recurrent notions, a single,
blank figure which is exclusively that of *outcome;* what I
live in such complicity with is the hallucination of *another
role:* the role of someone who "gets out."
Thus is revealed, once again, the language-nature of the
amorous sentiment: every solution is pitilessly referred to
its one and only idea—i.e., to a verbal being; so that,
finally, being language, the idea of outcome adjusts itself
to the foreclosure of any outcome: the lover's discourse is
in a sense a series of No Exits.

2.　　The Idea is always a scene of pathos which I
imagine and by which I am moved; in short, a theater.
And it is the theatrical nature of the Idea from which I
benefit: this theater, of the stoic genre, magnifies me,
grants me stature. By *imagining* an extreme solution (i.e.,
a definitive one; i.e., a definite one), I produce a fiction, I
become an artist, I set a scene, I paint my exit; the Idea is

Diderot

seen, like the pregnant moment (pregnant = endowed with a strong, chosen meaning) of bourgeois drama: sometimes this is a farewell scene, sometimes a formal letter, sometimes, for much later on, a dignified reencounter. The art of the catastrophe calms me down.

3.　　All the solutions I imagine are internal to the amorous system: withdrawal, travel, suicide, it is always the lover who sequesters himself, goes away, or dies; if he sees himself sequestered, departed, or dead, what he sees is always a lover: I order myself to be still in love and to

double bind

be no longer in love. This kind of identity of the problem and its solution precisely defines the *trap:* I am trapped because it lies outside my reach to change systems: I am "done for" twice over: inside my own system and because I cannot substitute another system for it. This double noose apparently defines a certain type of madness (the trap closes when the disaster is without contrary: "For there to

Schiller

be a misfortune, the good itself must do harm"). Puzzle: to "get out," I must get out of the system—which I want to get out of, etc. If it were not in the "nature" of amorous madness to pass, to cease of itself, no one could ever put an end to it (it is not because he is dead that Werther has stopped being in love, quite the contrary).

DOUBLE BIND: "Situation in which the subject cannot win, whatever he may do: heads I win, tails you lose" (Bettelheim).

Jealousy

jalousie / jealousy

"A sentiment which is born in love and which is produced by the fear that the loved person prefers someone else" (Littré).

Werther

1. The jealous man in the novel is not Werther but Herr Schmidt, Frederika's fiancé, the bad-tempered man. Werther's jealousy derives from images (seeing Albert slip his arm around Charlotte's waist), not from thought. This is because what is involved (and here is one of the book's beauties) is a tragic disposition, not a psychological one. Werther does not hate Albert; quite simply, Albert occupies a desired place: he is an adversary (a rival), not an enemy: he is not "odious." In his letters to Wilhelm, Werther shows himself to be anything but jealous. It is only when confidence is exchanged for the final narrative that the rivalry becomes acute, acrimonious, as if jealousy appeared in this simple transition from *I* to *he,* from an imaginary discourse (saturated by the other) to a discourse of the Other—of which Narrative is the statutory voice.

Proust

Tallemant

The Proustian narrator has little relation to Werther. Is he even a lover? He is merely jealous; in him, nothing "lunar"—except when he loves, in the fashion of a lover, the Mother (his grandmother).

TALLEMANT DES RÉAUX: Louis XIII: "His loves were strange loves: he had nothing of the lover about him but jealousy" (*Historiettes*).

2.   Werther is captured by this image: Charlotte cutting bread-and-butter and distributing the slices to her brothers and sisters. Charlotte is a cake, and this cake is divided up: each has his slice: I am not the only one—I am alone in nothing, I have brothers, sisters, I am to share, I must yield to the law of division: are not the goddesses of Destiny also the goddesses of the human Lot, of allotment—the Moirai, the last of whom is the Silent One, Death? Further, if I do not accept the partitioning out of love, I deny love's perfection, for it is proper to perfection to be shared: Melitta is shared because she is perfect, and Hyperion suffers from the fact: "My misery was truly limitless. I was forced to withdraw." Thus I suffer twice over: from the division itself, and from my incapacity to endure its nobility.

Hölderlin

3.   "When I love, I am very exclusive," Freud says (whom we shall take here for the paragon of normality). To be jealous is to conform. To reject jealousy ("to be perfect") is therefore to transgress a law. Zuleika has tried to seduce Joseph, and her husband is not distressed by her doing so; this scandal requires an explanation: the scene takes place in Egypt and Egypt is under a zodiacal sign which excludes jealousy: Gemini.
(Inverted conformism: one is no longer jealous, one condemns exclusivity, one lives with several lovers, etc.—though consider what is actually the case here: suppose I were forcing myself not to be jealous any longer, because I

Freud

Djedidi

FREUD: *Letters.*
DJEDIDI: *La Poésie amoureuse des Arabes:* Zuleika succeeds "somewhat." Joseph yielded "to the extent of a mosquito's wing," so that the legend could not put his virility in doubt.

etymology | was ashamed to be jealous? Jealousy is ugly, is bourgeois: it is an unworthy fuss, a *zeal*—and it is this zeal which I reject.)

4.   As a jealous man, I suffer four times over: because I am jealous, because I blame myself for being so, because I fear that my jealousy will wound the other, because I allow myself to be subject to a banality: I suffer from being excluded, from being aggressive, from being crazy, and from being common.

ETYMOLOGY: ζῆλος (*zêlos*)—zelosus—*jaloux* (the French word is borrowed from the troubadours).

I Love You

je-t'-aime / I-love-you

The figure refers not to the declaration of love, to
the avowal, but to the repeated utterance of the
love cry.

1.　　Once the first avowal has been made, *"I love you"*
has no meaning whatever; it merely repeats in an enigmatic mode—so blank does it appear—the old message
(which may not have been transmitted in these words). I
repeat it exclusive of any pertinence; it comes out of the
language, it divagates—where?

I could not decompose the expression without laughing.
Then there would be "me" on one side, "you" on the
other, and in between a joint of *reasonable* (i.e., lexical)
affection. Anyone can feel how much such a decomposi-
tion, though conforming to linguistic theory, would dis-
figure what is *flung out* in a single impulse. *To love* does
not exist in the infinitive (except by a metalinguistic
artifice): the subject and the object come to the word even
as it is uttered, and *I-love-you* must be understood (and
read here) in the Hungarian fashion, for instance, for
Hungarian uses a single word, *szeretlek,* as if French,
renouncing its splendid analytical quality, were an aggluti-
native language (and it is, indeed, agglutination which is
in question here). This clump is shattered by the slightest
syntactical alteration; it is, so to speak, beyond syntax and
yields itself to no structural transformation; it has no
equivalent among its substitutes, whose combination
might nonetheless produce the same meaning; I can say *I-*

R.H.

R.H.: Conversation.

love-you for days on end without perhaps ever being able to proceed to *"I love her"*: I resist making the other pass through a syntax, a predication, a language (the sole Assumption of *I-love-you* is to apostrophize it, to give it the expansion of a first name: *Ariadne, I love you,* Dionysus says).

Nietzsche

2.   *I-love-you* has no usages. Like a child's word, it enters into no social constraint; it can be a sublime, solemn, trivial word, it can be an erotic, pornographic word. It is a socially irresponsible word.

I-love-you is without nuance. It suppresses explanations, adjustments, degrees, scruples. In a way—exorbitant paradox of language—to say *I-love-you* is to proceed as if there were no theater of speech, and this word is always *true* (has no other referent than its utterance: it is a performative).

I-love-you has no "elsewhere"—it is the word of the (maternal, amorous) dyad; in it, no distance, no distortion will split the sign; it is the metaphor of nothing *else*.

Lacan

I-love-you is not a sentence: it does not transmit a meaning, but fastens onto a limit situation: "the one where the subject is suspended in a specular relation to the other." It is a holophrase.

(Though spoken billions of times, *I-love-you* is extra-lexicographical; it is a figure whose definition cannot transcend the heading.)

3.   The word (the word-as-sentence) has a meaning only at the moment I utter it; there is no other information

LACAN: See *Le Séminaire,* I, on the limit situation and the holophrase.

in it but its immediate saying: no reservoir, no armory of
meaning. Everything is in the speaking of it: it is a
"formula," but this formula corresponds to no ritual; the
situations in which I say *I-love-you* cannot be classified: *I-
love-you* is irrepressible and unforeseeable Then to what
linguistic order does this odd being, this linguistic feint,
belong, too articulated to be no more than an impulse, too
phatic to be a sentence? It is neither quite what is uttered
(no message is congealed, sorted, mummified within it,
ready for dissection) nor quite the uttering itself (the subject does not allow himself to be intimidated by the play of
interlocutory sites). We might call it a *proffering,* which
has no scientific place: *I-love-you* belongs neither in the
realm of linguistics nor in that of semiology. Its occasion
(the point of departure for speaking it) would be, rather,
Music. In the manner of what happens in singing, in the
proffering of *I-love-you,* desire is neither repressed (as in
what is uttered) nor recognized (where we did not expect
it: as in the uttering itself) but simply: released, as an
orgasm. Orgasm is not spoken, but it speaks and it says: *I-
love-you.* ~~DOES~~ DID YOU LOVE EVERYONE
IN THIS CASE.

4.   To *I-love-you* there are various mundane
answers: "I don't love *you,*" "I don't believe a word,"
"Why do you have to say so?," etc. But the true dismissal
is: "There is no answer": I am wiped out more completely
if I am rejected not only as the one who demands but also
as the speaking subject (as such, I have at least the
mastery of the formulas); it is my language, the last resort
of my existence, which is denied, not my demand; as for
the demand, I can wait, make it again, present it later; but
denied the power of questioning, I am "dead," forever.
"There is no answer," the Mother makes Françoise say to

Proust

the young Proustian narrator, who then correctly identifies
himself with the "mistress" sent away by her lover's con-
cierge: the Mother is not forbidden, she is foreclosed and
I go mad.

5.   *I love you. —So do I.*

So do I is not a perfect answer, for what is perfect can
only be formal, and the form here is deficient, in that it
does not literally take up the proffering—and it is proper
to the proffering to be literal. However, insofar as it is
assimilated into the subject's hallucination, this reply is
enough to set going a whole discourse of jubilation: jubilation all the more powerful in that it wells up by means of
a sudden transformation: Saint-Preux discovers abruptly,
Rousseau after several haughty denials, that Julie loves him. This is
the delirious truth which does not come by reasoning, by
any slow preparation, but by surprise, awakening (*satori*),
Proust conversion. The Proustian child—asking that his mother
sleep in his room—wants to obtain the *So-do-I:* wants to
deliriously, in the fashion of a madman; and he, too, obtains it by a reversal, by the Father's capricious decision,
conceding him the Mother ("Tell Françoise to make up
your bed in his room, then, and sleep there tonight").

6.   I hallucinate what is *empirically* impossible: that
our two profferings be made *at the same time:* that one
does not follow the other, as if it depended on it. Proffering cannot be double (doubled): only the *single flash* will
do, in which two forces join (separate, divided, they
would not exceed some ordinary agreement). For the

PROUST: *Swann's Way.*

single flash achieves this unheard-of thing: the abolition of all responsibility. Exchange, gift, and theft (the only known forms of economy) each in its way implies heterogeneous objects and a dislocated time: my desire against something else—and this always requires the time for drawing up the agreement. Simultaneous proffering establishes a movement whose model is socially unknown, unthinkable: neither exchange, nor gift, nor theft, our proffering, welling up in crossed fires, designates an expenditure which relapses nowhere and whose very community abolishes any thought of reservation: we enter each by means of the other into absolute materialism.

7. *So-do-I* inaugurates a mutation: the old rules fall away, everything is possible—even, then, this: that I give up possessing you.
A revolution, in short—not so far, perhaps, from the political kind: for, in both cases, what I hallucinate is the absolute New: (amorous) reform has no appeal for me. And, to cap the paradox, this pure New is ultimately the most worn-down of stereotypes (just last night, I heard it uttered in a play by Sagan: every other night, on TV, someone says: *I love you*).

8. —And what if I didn't interpret *I-love-you?* What if I maintained the proffering on this side of the symptom? —You take your chances: haven't you said hundreds of times how intolerable the lover's suffering is, and his necessity to get out of it? If you want to "recover," you have to believe in the symptoms, and believe that *I-love-you* is one of them; you have to interpret, i.e., ultimately you have to *disparage*.

BAUDELAIRE: *"La Mort des amants."*

—Then what do we have to think of suffering? How do we have to conceive it? evaluate it? Is suffering necessarily on the side of evil? Doesn't suffering in love have to do only with a reactive, disparaging treatment (one must submit to the prohibition)? Can one, reversing the evaluation, imagine a tragic view of love's suffering, a tragic affirmation of *I-love-you?* And if (amorous) love were put (put back) under the sign of the Active?

9.　　　Whence a new view of *I-love-you.* Not as a symptom but as an action. I speak so that you may answer, and the scrupulous form (the letter) of the answer will assume an effective value, in the manner of a formula. Hence it is not enough that the other should answer me with a mere signified, however positive (*"So do I"*): the addressed subject must take the responsibility of formulating, of proffering the *I-love-you* which I extend: *I love you,* Pelléas says. —*I love you, too,* Mélisande says.

Pelléas's imperious suit (supposing that Mélisande's answer was *exactly* the one he expected, which is probable since he dies immediately afterwards) proceeds from the necessity, for the amorous subject, not only to be loved in return, to know it, to be sure of it, etc. (all operations which do not exceed the level of the signified), but to *hear it said* in the form which is as affirmative, as complete, as articulated as his own; what I want is to receive full in the face, entirely, literally, without evasion or leakage, the formula, the archetype of love's word: no syntactical subterfuge, no variation: that the two phrases, the two words, should correspond totally, coinciding signifier by signifier (*So do I* would be just the contrary of a holophrase); what matters is the physical, bodily, labial proffering of the word: open your lips and let it out (be obscene).

What I want, deliriously, is to *obtain the word*. Magical,
mythical? The Beast—held enchanted in his ugliness—
loves Beauty; Beauty, obviously, does not love the Beast,
but at the end, vanquished (unimportant by what; let us
say by the *conversations* she has with the Beast), she, too,
says the magic word: *"Je vous aime, la Bête";* and immediately, through the sumptuous arpeggio of a harp, a
new subject appears. Is this story an archaic one? Then
here is another: a man suffers because his wife has left
him; he wants her to come back, he wants—specifically—
her to say *I love you* to him, and he, too, runs after the
words; finally she says it to him: whereupon he faints dead
away: a film made in 1975. And then, once again, the
myth: the Flying Dutchman wanders the earth in search of
the word; if he obtains it (by an oath of fidelity), he will
cease wandering (what matters to the myth is not the rule
of fidelity but its proffering, its song).

Ravel

10.   Singular encounter (within the German language): one and the same word (*Bejahung*) for two
affirmations: one, seized upon by psychoanalysis, is
doomed to disparagement (the child's first affirmation
must be denied so that there may be access to the unconscious); the other, posited by Nietzsche, is a mode of the
will-to-power (nothing psychological, and even less of the
social in it), the production of difference, the *yes* of this
affirmation becomes innocent (it contains the reaction-
formation): this is the *amen*.

I-love-you is active. It affirms itself as force—against
other forces. Which ones? The thousand forces of the
world, which are, all of them, disparaging forces (science,
doxa, reality, reason, etc.). Or again: against language.
Just as the *amen* is at the limit of language, without collu-

RAVEL: *"Les entretiens de la Belle et de la Bête,"* from *Ma Mère l'Oye.*

sion with its system, stripping it of its "reactive mantle," so the proffering of love (*I-love-you*) stands at the limit of syntax, welcomes tautology (*I-love-you* means *I-love-you*), rejects the servility of the Sentence (it is merely a holophrase). As proffering, *I-love-you* is not a sign, but plays against the signs. The one who does not say *I-love-you* (between whose lips *I-love-you* is reluctant to pass) is condemned to emit the many uncertain, doubting, greedy signs of love, its indices, its "proofs": gestures, looks, sighs, allusions, ellipses: he must let himself be *interpreted;* he is dominated by the reactive occasion of love's signs, exiled into the servile world of language *in that he does not say everything* (the slave is one who has his tongue cut off, who can speak only by looks, expressions, faces).

The "signs" of love feed an enormous reactive literature: love is *represented,* entrusted to an aesthetic of appearances (it is Apollo, *ultimately,* who writes every love story). As a counter-sign, *I-love-you* is on the side of Dionysus: suffering is not denied (nor even complaint, disgust, resentment), but by its proffering, it is not internalized: to say *I-love-you* (to repeat it) is to expel the reaction-formation, to return it to the deaf and doleful world of signs—of the detours of speech (which, however, I never cease to pass through). As proffering, *I-love-you* is on the side of expenditure. Those who seek the proffering of the word (lyric poets, liars, wanderers) are subjects of Expenditure: they spend the word, as if it were impertinent (base) that it be recovered somewhere; they are at the extreme limit of language, where language itself (and who else would do so in its place?) recognizes that it is without backing or guarantee, working without a net.

Nietzsche

NIETZSCHE: This entire fragment, of course, takes its departure from Deleuze's *Nietzsche et la philosophie.*

Love's Languor

langueur / languor

Subtle state of amorous desire, experienced in its
dearth, outside of any will-to-possess.

1.　　The Satyr says: I want my desire to be satisfied
immediately. If I see a sleeping face, parted lips, an open
hand, I want to be able *to hurl myself upon them*. This
Satyr—figure of the Immediate—is the very contrary of
the Languorous. In languor, I merely wait: "I knew no
end to desiring you." (Desire is everywhere, but in the
amorous state it becomes something very special:
languor.)

Sollers

2.　　"and you tell me my other self will you answer me
at last I am tired of you I want you I dream of you for you
against you answer me your name is a perfume about me
your color bursts among the thorns bring back my heart
with cool wine make me a coverlet of the morning I
suffocate beneath this mask withered shrunken skin nothing exists save desire"

Sappho

3.　　". . . for when I glance at you even an instant, I
can no longer utter a word: my tongue thickens to a lump,
and beneath my skin breaks out a subtle fire: my eyes are
blind, my ears filled with humming, and sweat streams
down my body, I am seized by a sudden shuddering; I turn

SOLLERS: *Paradis*.

greener than grass, and in a moment more, I feel I shall die."

Symposium

Werther

Ruysbroeck

Freud

cortezia

4.   "My soul, when I embraced Agathon, came to my lips, as if the wretch would leave me and go elsewhere." In amorous languor, something keeps going away; it is as if desire were nothing but this hemorrhage. Such is amorous fatigue: a hunger not to be satisfied, a gaping love. Or again: my entire self is drawn, transferred to the loved object which takes its place: languor would be that exhausting transition from narcissistic libido to object libido. (Desire for the absent being and desire for the present being: languor superimposes the two desires, putting absence within presence. Whence a state of contradiction: this is the "gentle fire.")

SYMPOSIUM: Plato to Agathon.
WERTHER: "The wretch whose life gradually dies away in a disease of languor nothing can check."
RUYSBROECK: "When the creature has risen, offering what it can, without attaining what it would, then is born the spiritual languor."
FREUD: "It is only in the fulfillment of amorous states that most of the libido is transferred to the object and that this latter takes the place, to a certain degree, of the ego" (*Outline of Psychoanalysis*).
CORTEZIA: Quoted by Denis de Rougemont, *Love in the Western World*.

The Love Letter

lettre / letter

This figure refers to the special dialectic of the
love letter, both blank (encoded) and expressive
(charged with longing to signify desire).

Werther

1.   When Werther (in the Ambassador's employ)
writes to Charlotte, his letter follows this outline: 1. What
joy to be thinking of you! 2. Here I am in a mundane
situation, and without you I feel utterly alone. 3. I have
met someone (Fraülein von B . . .) who resembles
you and with whom I can speak of you. 4. I keep hoping
that we can be reunited. —A single piece of information is
varied, in the manner of a musical theme: *I am thinking
of you.*

What does "thinking of you" mean? It means: forgetting
"you" (without forgetting, life itself is not possible) and
frequently waking out of that forgetfulness. Many things,

Freud

by association, bring you back into my discourse. "Thinking of you" means precisely this metonymy. For, in itself,
such thinking is blank: I do not think *you;* I simply make
you recur (to the very degree that I forget you). It is this
form (this rhythm) which I call "thought": *I have nothing
to tell you,* save that it is to you that I tell this nothing:

Goethe

Why do I turn once again to writing?
Beloved, you must not ask such a question,
For the truth is, I have nothing to tell you,
All the same, your dear hands will hold this note.

FREUD: To his fiancée: "Oh, that gardener Bünslow! How lucky he is to
be able to shelter my beloved" (*Letters*).
GOETHE: Quoted by Freud.

Gide

("Think of Hubert, writes the narrator of *Paludes,* that Book of Nothing, on his engagement calendar, comically enough.)

2.   "As you see," writes the Marquise de Merteuil, "when you write someone, it is for that person and not for yourself, so you must be sure not to say what you think, but rather what will please that person." The Marquise is not in love; what she postulates is a *correspondence,* i.e., a **A.C.** tactical enterprise to defend positions, make conquests; this enterprise must reconnoiter the positions (the subgroups) of the adverse group, i.e., must articulate the other's image in various points which the letter will try to touch (in this sense, "correspondence" is precisely the word to use, in its mathematical sense). But for the lover the letter has no tactical value: it is purely *expressive*—at most, flattering (but here flattery is not a matter of self-interest, merely the language of devotion); what I engage in with the other is a *relation,* not a correspondence: the relation brings together two images. You are everywhere, your image is total, Werther writes to Charlotte, in various ways.

3.   Like desire, the love letter waits for an answer; it implicitly enjoins the other to reply, for without a reply the other's image changes, becomes *other.* This is what the **Freud** young Freud explains so authoritatively to his fiancée: "Yet I don't want my letters to keep remaining unanswered, and I shall stop writing you altogether if you don't

GIDE: *Paludes.*
LACLOS: *Les Liaisons dangereuses.*
A.C.: Conversation.
FREUD: *Letters.*

write back. Perpetual monologues apropos of a loved
being, which are neither corrected nor nourished by that
being, lead to erroneous notions concerning mutual relations, and make us strangers to each other when we meet
again, so that we find things different from what, without
realizing it, we imagined."

(The one who would accept the "injustices" of communication, the one who would continue speaking lightly,
tenderly, without being answered, would acquire a great
mastery: the mastery of the Mother.)

The Loquela

loquela

This word, borrowed from Ignatius of Loyola, designates the flux of language through which the subject tirelessly rehashes the effects of a wound or the consequences of an action: an emphatic form of the lover's discourse.

16th-century song

Schubert

Greek

1. *Trop penser me font amours*—love makes me think too much. At times, result of some infinitesimal stimulus, a fever of language overcomes me, a parade of reasons, interpretations, pronouncements. I am aware of nothing but a machine running all by itself, a hurdy-gurdy whose crank is turned by a staggering but anonymous bystander, and which is never silent. In the *loquela,* nothing ever manages to prevent these repetitions. Once I happen to produce a "successful" phrase in my mind (imagining I have found the right expression for some truth or other), it becomes a formula I repeat in proportion to the relief it affords (finding the right word is euphoric); I chew it over, feeding on it; like children or the victims of merycism, I keep swallowing and regurgitating my wound. I spin, unwind and weave the lover's case, and begin all over again (these are the meanings of the verb μηρύομαι, *meruomaī:* to spin, to unwind, to weave).

Or again: the autistic child frequently watches his own fingers touching objects (but does not watch the objects

SCHUBERT: Barefoot on the ice, he staggers along, and his bowl is always empty. No one listens to him, no one looks at him, and the dogs growl at the old man. But he pays no heed, walking on and turning his crank, the hurdy-gurdy never still (*"Der Leiermann," Die Winterreise,* poems by Müller).

Bettelheim

themselves): this is *twiddling,* which is not a form of play but a ritual manipulation, marked by stereotyped and compulsive features. As with the lover suffering from the *loquela:* he twiddles his wound.

2.　　Humboldt calls the sign's freedom *volubility.* I am (inwardly) voluble, because I cannot anchor my discourse: the signs turn "in free wheeling." If I could constrain the sign, submit it to some sanction, I could find rest at last. If only we could put our minds in plaster casts, like our legs! But I cannot keep from thinking, from speaking; no director is there to interrupt the interior movie I keep making of myself, someone to shout, *Cut!* Volubility is a kind of specifically human misery: I am language-mad: no one listens to me, no one looks at me, but (like Schubert's organ-grinder) I go on talking, turning my hurdy-gurdy.

3.　　I take a role: I am *the one who is going to cry;* and I play this role for myself, and *it makes me cry:* I am my own theater. And seeing me cry this way makes me cry all the more; and if the tears tend to decrease, I quickly repeat to myself the lacerating phrase that will set them flowing again. I have two speakers in myself, busy *raising the tone,* from one utterance to the next, as in the old stichomythias: there is a bliss in doubled, in redoubled speech, taken to the final din (the clown scene).

Werther

(I. Werther delivers a tirade against bad temper: "Tears come to his eyes."

BETTELHEIM: *The Empty Fortress.*

162

II. He describes in Charlotte's presence a scene of funereal leave-taking; his narrative overwhelms him with its violence and he wipes his eyes with his handkerchief.

III. Werther writes to Charlotte, describing to her the image of his eventual grave: "And now I am crying like a child, telling you all this so vividly."

Hugo

IV. "At twenty, Mme Desbordes-Valmore says, severe pains forced me to give up singing, because my own voice made me cry.")

HUGO: *Pierres.*

The Last Leaf

magie / magic
Magic consultations, secret rites, and votive
actions are not absent from the amorous subject's
life, whatever culture he belongs to.

Schubert

1. "Here and there, on the trees, some leaves remain.
And I often stand deep in thought before them. I contem-
plate a leaf and attach my hope to it. When the wind plays
with the leaf, I tremble in every limb. And if it should fall,
alas, my hope falls with it."

In order to be able to question fate, there must be an
alternative: she loves me / she loves me not; we require
an object capable of a simple variation (*will fall / won't
fall*) and an external force (divinity, chance, wind) which
marks one of the poles of the variation. I always ask the
same question (will I be loved?), and this question is an
alternative: *all or nothing;* I do not suppose that things
can develop, be exempted from desire's *a propos.* I am not
dialectical. Dialectic would say: the leaf will not fall, and
then it will fall; but meanwhile you will have changed and
you will no longer ask yourself the question.

(From any consultant whatever, I expect the following:
"The person you love loves you as well, and will tell you
so tonight.")

2. Sometimes the anxiety is so powerful and so press-
ing (since that is the word's etymology)—an anxiety of

SCHUBERT: *"Letzte Hoffnung," Die Winterreise.*

waiting, for instance—that it becomes necessary to *do something*. This "something" is naturally (ancestrally) a vow: *if* (you come back . . .), *then* (I will fulfill my vow).

X confides: "The first time; he lit a candle in a little Italian church. He was surprised by the flame's beauty, and the action seemed less absurd. Why henceforth deprive himself of the pleasure of creating a light? So he began again, attaching to this delicate gesture (tilting the new candle toward the one already lit, gently rubbing their wicks, taking pleasure when the fire 'took,' filling his eyes with that intimate yet brilliant light) ever vaguer vows which were to include—for fear of choosing—'everything which fails in the world.' "

"I am odious"

monstreux / monstrous

The subject suddenly realizes that he is
imprisoning the loved object in a net of tyrannies:
he has been pitiable, now he becomes monstrous.

Plato

1.   In Plato's *Phaedrus,* the speeches of Lysias the
Sophist and of the early Socrates (before the latter makes
his recantation) rest on this principle: that the lover is
intolerable (by his heaviness) to the beloved. There follows the catalogue of importunate features: the lover cannot bear anyone to be superior or equal to himself in his
beloved's eyes, and strives to defeat every rival; he keeps
the beloved apart from a host of relationships; he attempts, by a thousand indelicate schemes, to keep the beloved in ignorance, so that he will know only what comes
to him from his lover; he secretly craves the loss of what is
dearest to the beloved: father, mother, relatives, friends;
he wants the beloved to have neither home nor children;
his daily assiduity is wearisome; he is not content to be
left alone for a minute, day or night; though old (which in
itself is importunate), he acts as a tyrannical detective and
constantly subjects the beloved to malicious spying, while
he himself subjects himself to no such prohibitions, later
on, as to infidelity and ingratitude. Whatever he supposes,
the lover's heart is filled with bad feelings: his love is not
generous.

2.   The lover's discourse stifles the other, who finds no
place for his own language beneath this massive utterance.

It is not that I keep the other from speaking; but I know how to *make the pronouns skid:* "I speak and you hear me, hence we exist" (Ponge). Sometimes, in terror, I become aware of this reversal: I who supposed myself to be pure subject (subjected subject: fragile, delicate, pitiable) find myself turned into an obtuse thing blindly moving onward, crushing everything beneath his discourse; I who love am undesirable, consigned to the category of the bores: the ones who bear down too hard, who irritate, encroach, complicate, demand, intimidate (or more simply: those who speak). I have monumentally deceived myself.

(The other is disfigured by his persistent silence, as in those terrible dreams in which a loved person shows up with the lower part of his face quite erased, without any mouth at all; and I, the one who speaks, I too am disfigured: soliloquy makes me into a monster: one huge tongue.

No Answer

mutisme / silence

The amorous subject suffers anxiety because the loved object replies scantily or not at all to his language (discourse or letters).

1.   "When you were talking to him, discussing any subject at all, X frequently seemed to be looking away, listening to something else: you broke off, discouraged; after a long silence, X would say: 'Go on, I'm listening to you'; then you resumed as best you could the thread of a story in which you no longer believed."

(Like a bad concert hall, affective space contains dead spots where the sound fails to circulate. —The perfect interlocutor, the friend, is he not the one who constructs around you the greatest possible resonance? Cannot friendship be defined as a space with total sonority?)

2.   This evasive listening, which I can capture only after some delay, involves me in a sordid calculation: desperately trying to seduce, to divert, I imagined that by talking I was lavishing treasures of ingenuity, but these treasures have produced only indifference; I am spending my "qualities" for nothing: a whole program of affects, doctrines, awareness, and delicacy, all the brilliance my ego can command dies away, muffled in an inert space, as if—culpable thought—my quality exceeded that of the loved object, as if I were *in advance* of that object. Now,

the affective relation is an exact machine; coincidence, *perfect pitch* in the musical sense are fundamental to it; what is out of phase is immediately *de trop:* my language is not, strictly speaking, a discard but rather an "overstock": what is not consumed in the moment (in the movement) and is therefore remaindered.

(This distracted kind of listening generates an anxiety of decisions: should I continue, go on talking "in the void"? This would require precisely the assurance which amorous sensibility does not permit. Should I stop, give up? This would seem to show anger, accusation of the other, producing a "scene." The trap all over again.)

3.   "This is what death is, most of all: everything that has been seen, will have been seen for nothing. Mourning over what we have perceived." In those brief moments when I speak for nothing, it is as if I were dying. For the loved being becomes a leaden figure, a dream creature *who does not speak,* and silence, in dreams, is death. Or again: the gratifying Mother shows me the Mirror, the Image, and says to me: "That's you." But the silent Mother does not tell me what I am: I am no longer established, I drift painfully, without existence.

François Wahl

Freud

FRANÇOIS WAHL: *"Chute."*
FREUD: "The Three Caskets."

Clouds

nuages / clouds

Meaning and employment of that darkening of
mood which overtakes the subject under various
circumstances.

Werther

1.   Werther is kind to Frederika, the daughter of the
pastor of St *** to whom he and Charlotte pay a visit.
The face of Herr Schmidt, Frederika's fiancé, darkens
accordingly; he refuses to take part in the conversation.
Werther then expatiates on bad humor; it stems from our
jealousy, our vanity, it is a discontent with ourselves
which we project onto others, etc. "Show me the man,
Werther says, who has the honesty and the honor to conceal his bad humor, to endure it in solitude, without de-
stroying the pleasure of those around him!" Such a man is
obviously not to be found, for bad humor is nothing more
or less than a message. Unable to be obviously jealous
without certain disadvantages, among which absurdity, I
shift my jealousy, I produce only a derived, a distorted,
indeed an incomplete effect, whose actual motive is not
openly spoken: incapable of concealing the wound and
not daring to declare its cause, I compromise; I botch the
content without renouncing the form; the result of this
transaction is *temper,* which offers itself to a reading like
the index of a sign: *here you should read* (that something
is awry): I simply lay my pathos down on the table, re-
serving to myself the right to unwrap the package later,
depending on the circumstances: either I reveal myself (in
the course of an "explanation"), or else I swathe myself

J.-L.B.

still further (such moods are a short circuit between the state and the sign). (Misreading: Werther attacks bad humor in that it weighs on those around you; yet, later on, he himself will commit suicide, surely a heavier burden. Is a love suicide perhaps an exacerbated temper, a kind of tantrum?)

2.   So much for bad humor: a crude sign, a shameful blackmail. Yet there are subtler clouds, all the tenuous shadows of swift and uncertain source which pass across the relationship, changing its light and its modeling; suddenly it is another landscape, a faint black intoxication. The cloud, then, is no more than this: *I'm missing something*. Summarily I inventory the states of dearth by which Zen has encoded human sensibility (*furyu*): solitude (*sabi*), the sadness which overcomes me because of the "incredible naturalness" of things (*wabi*), nostalgia (*aware*), the sentiment of strangeness (*yugen*). "I am happy but I am sad": such was Mélisande's "cloud."

Zen

Pelléas

J.-L.B.: Conversation.

"And the night illuminated the night"

nuit / night

Any state which provokes in the subject the metaphor of the darkness, whether affective, intellective, or existential, in which he struggles or subsides.

John of the Cross

1. I experience alternately two nights, one good, the other bad. To express this, I borrow a mystical distinction: *estar a oscuras* (to be in the dark) can occur without there being any blame to attach, since I am deprived of the light of causes and effects; *estar en tinieblas* (to be in the shadows: *tenebrae*) happens to me when I am blinded by attachment to things and the disorder which emanates from that condition.

Most often I am in the very darkness of my desire; I know not what it wants, good itself is an evil to me, everything resounds, I live between blows, my head ringing: *estoy en tinieblas*. But sometimes, too, it is another Night: alone, in a posture of meditation (perhaps a role I assign myself?), I think quite calmly about the other, as the other is; I suspend any interpretation; I enter into the night of non-meaning; desire continues to vibrate (the darkness is transluminous), but there is nothing I want to grasp; this is the Night of non-profit, of subtle, invisible expenditure: *estoy a oscuras:* I am here, sitting simply and calmly in the dark interior of love.

Ruysbroeck

2.   The second night envelops the first, the Darkness illuminates the Shadows: "And the night was dark and it illuminated the night." I make no attempt to emerge from the amorous impasse by Decision, Enterprise, Separation, Sacrifice, etc.; in short, *by gesture*. I merely substitute one night for the other. "To darken this darkness, this is the gate of all wonder."

John of the Cross

Tao

JOHN OF THE CROSS: *"Admirable cosa que siendo tenebrosa alumbrase la noche."*
TAO: "Non-Being and Being, emerging from a single ground, are differentiated only by their names. This single ground is called Darkness. —To darken this darkness, that is the gate of all wonder" (*Tao Te Ching*).

The Ribbon

objets / objects

Every object touched by the loved being's body becomes part of that body, and the subject eagerly attaches himself to it.

Werther

1. Werther multiplies the gestures of fetishism: he kisses the knot of ribbon Charlotte has given him for his birthday, the letter she sends him (even putting the sand to his lips), the pistols she has touched. From the loved being emanates a power nothing can stop and which will impregnate everything it comes in contact with, even if only by a glance: if Werther, unable to go see Charlotte, sends her his servant, it is this servant himself upon whom her eyes have rested who becomes for Werther a part of Charlotte ("I would have taken his head between my hands and kissed him then and there, had not human respect prevented me"). Each object thus consecrated (placed within the influence of the god) becomes like the stone of Bologna, which by night gives off the rays it has accumulated during the day.

Lacan

(He puts the Phallus in place of the Mother—identifies himself with it. Werther wants to be buried with the ribbon Charlotte has given him; in the grave, he lies alongside the Mother—then specifically evoked.)

Sometimes the metonymic object is a presence (engendering joy); sometimes it is an absence (engendering distress). What does my reading of it depend on? —If I believe myself about to be gratified, the object will be favorable; if I see myself as abandoned, it will be sinister.

2.　　　Aside from these fetishes, there is no other object in the amorous world. It is a world sensuously impoverished, abstract, erased, canceled out; my gaze passes through things without acknowledging their seduction; I am dead to all sensuality except that of the "charming body." Of the external world, the only thing I can associate with my condition is the quality of the weather, as if the day's character were a dimension of the Image-repertoire (the Image is neither profound nor colored, but it is charged with all the nuances of light and warmth, communicating with the amorous body, which thus feels itself to be well or ill as a whole, as a communion). In the code of the Japanese haiku, there must always be a word which refers back to the time of day and of the year; this is the *kigo,* the season-word. Amorous notation retains the *kigo,* that faint allusion to the rain, to the evening, to the light, to everything that envelops, diffuses.

haiku

Love's Obscenity

obscène / obscene

Discredited by modern opinion, love's sentimentality must be assumed by the amorous subject as a powerful transgression which leaves him alone and exposed; by a reversal of values, then, it is this sentimentality which today constitutes love's obscenity.

1.   Example of obscenity: each occasion in this very text that the word "love" is used (the obscenity would cease if we were to say, mockingly, "luv").

Lacan

Or again: "Evening at the Opera: a very bad tenor comes on stage; in order to express his love to the woman he loves, who is beside him, he stands facing the public. I am this tenor: like a huge animal, obscene and stupid, brightly lighted as in a show window, I declaim an elaborately encoded aria, without looking at the one I love, to whom I am supposed to be addressing myself."

Or again: a dream: I am giving a course "on" love; my students are all women, no longer young: I am Paul Géraldy.

Or again: ". . . the word did not seem to him to repay such frequent repetition. The slippery monosyllable, with its lingual and labial, and the bleating vowel between—it came to sound positively offensive; it suggested watered milk, or anything else that was pale and insipid . . ."

Thomas
Mann

Or finally: my love is "a sexual organ of unparalleled sensitivity which trembles as it makes me utter terrible

THOMAS MANN: *The Magic Mountain.*

Bataille

cries, the cries of a huge but stinking ejaculation, at grips with the ecstatic gift that one makes of oneself as a naked, obscene victim . . . mocked by the loud laughter of the whores."

I take for myself the scorn lavished on any kind of pathos: formerly, in the name of reason ("In order that so ardent a production, Lessing said of *Werther,* not do more harm than good, do you not suppose it required a brief, cool peroration?"), today in the name of "modernity," which acknowledges a subject, provided it be "generalized" ("True popular music, the music of the masses, plebeian music, is open to all the impulses of *group subjectivities,* no longer to the solitary subjectivity, the highfalutin senti- mental subjectivity of the isolated subject . . ." Daniel Charles, *"Musique et Oubli"*).

2.   Encounter with an intellectual in love: for him, "to assume" (not to repress) extreme stupidity, the naked stupidity of his discourse, is the same thing as for Bataille's subject to take off his clothes in a public place: the necessary form of the impossible and of the sovereign: an abjection such that no discourse of transgression can recuperate it and such that it exposes itself without protec- tion to the moralism of anti-morality. From this point, he judges his contemporaries as so many *innocents:* they are innocent, those who censure amorous sentimentality in the name of a new morality: "The distinctive mark of modern souls is not lying but *innocence,* incarnate in lying

Nietzsche

moralism. To discover this *innocence* everywhere—that may be the most disheartening part of our task."

GEORGES BATAILLE: *L'Oeil pinéal.*
NIETZSCHE: *On the Genealogy of Morals.*

(Historical reversal: it is no longer the sexual which is indecent, it is the *sentimental*—censured in the name of what is in fact only *another morality*.)

3.   The lover raves (he "shifts the sentiment of values"); but his raving is stupid. What is stupider than a lover? So stupid that no one dares offer his discourse publicly without a serious mediation: novel, play, or analysis (between tweezers). Socrates's *daimon* (the one who spoke first within him) whispered to him: *no*. My *daimon,* on the contrary, is my stupidity: like the Nietzschean ass, I say yes to everything, in the field of my love. I insist, reject all training, repeat the same actions; no one can educate me—nor can I educate myself; my discourse is continuously without reflection; I do not know how to reverse it, organize it, stud it with glances, quotation marks; I always speak *in the first degree;* I persist in a dutiful, discreet, conformist delirium, tamed and banalized by literature.

(What is stupid is to be surprised. The lover is constantly so; he has no time to transform, to reverse, to protect. Perhaps he knows his stupidity, but he *does not censure it.* Or again: his stupidity acts as a cleavage, a perversion: *it's stupid,* he says, *and yet . . . it's true.*)

4.   Whatever is anachronic is obscene. As a (modern) divinity, History is repressive, History forbids us to be out of time. Of the past we tolerate only the ruin, the monument, kitsch, what is *amusing:* we reduce this past to no more than its signature. The lover's sentiment is old-fashioned, but this antiquation cannot even be recuperated as

a spectacle: love falls outside of *interesting* time; no historical, polemical meaning can be given to it; it is in this that it is obscene.

5.   In amorous life, the fabric of incidents is of an incredible futility, and this futility, allied with the highest seriousness, is literally unseemly. When I seriously envisage committing suicide because of a telephone call that doesn't come, an obscenity occurs which is as great as when, in Sade, the pope sodomizes a turkey. But sentimental obscenity is less strange, and that is what makes it more abject; nothing can exceed the unseemliness of a subject who collapses in tears because his other behaves distantly, "when there are still so many men in the world who are dying of hunger, when so many nations are struggling for their freedom," etc.

Sade

6.   The moral tax levied by society on all transgressions affects passion still more than sex today. Everyone will understand that X has "huge problems" with his sexuality; but no one will be interested in those Y may have with his sentimentality: love is obscene precisely in that it puts the sentimental in place of the sexual. That "sentimental old baby" (Fourier) who suddenly died while deeply in love would seem as obscene as President Félix Faure, who died of a stroke in his mistress's arms.

7.   Amorous obscenity is extreme: nothing can redeem it, bestow upon it the positive value of a transgression; the subject's solitude is timid, stripped of any *décor:* no Bataille will give a style (an *écriture*) to that obscenity.

The amorous text (scarcely a text at all) consists of little narcissisms, psychological paltrinesses; it is without grandeur: or its grandeur (but who, *socially,* is present to acknowledge it?) is to be unable to reach any grandeur, not even that of "crass materialism." It is then the *impossible* moment when the obscene can really coincide with affirmation, with the *amen,* the limit of language (any utterable obscenity as such can no longer be the last degree of the obscene: uttering it, even through the wink of a figure, I myself am *already* recuperated, socialized).

In Praise of Tears

pleurer / crying

The amorous subject has a particular propensity
to cry: the functioning and appearance of tears
in this subject.

1.   The slightest amorous emotion, whether of happiness or of disappointment, brings Werther to tears.

Werther   Werther weeps often, very often, and in floods. Is it the
lover in Werther who weeps, or is it the romantic?

Is it perhaps a disposition proper to the amorous type, this
propensity to dissolve in tears? Subjected to the Image-
repertoire, he flouts the censure which today forbids the
adult tears and by which a man means to protest his
virility (Piaf's satisfaction and maternal tenderness:
"Mais vous pleurez, Milord!"). By releasing his tears
without constraint, he follows the orders of the amorous
body, which is a body in liquid expansion, a bathed body:
to weep together, to flow together: delicious tears finish
off the reading of Klopstock which Charlotte and Werther
perform together. Where does the lover obtain the right to
cry, if not in a reversal of values, of which the body is the
first target? He accepts rediscovering the *infant body*.

Schubert   Further, here, the amorous body is doubled by a historical
one. Who will write the history of tears? In which socie-
ties, in which periods, have we wept? Since when is it that
men (and not women) no longer cry? Why was "sensibil-

SCHUBERT: *"Lob der Tränen"* (In Praise of Tears), poem by A. W.
Schlegel.

ity," at a certain moment, transformed into "sentimental-ity"? The images of virility are shifting; the Greeks as well as our audiences of the seventeenth century cried a great deal at the theater. St. Louis, according to Michelet, suffered at not having received the gift of tears; on the one occasion that he felt tears running gently down his face, "they seemed to him delectable and comforting, not only to the heart but to the tongue." (Similarly: in 1199, a young monk set out for a Cistercian abbey in Brabant in order to obtain, by the tears of its inmates, the gift of tears.)

Michelet

(A Nietzschean problem: How do History and Type combine? Is it not up to the type to formulate—to form—what is out of time, ahistorical? In the lover's very tears, our society represses its own timelessness, thereby turning the weeping lover into a lost object whose repression is necessary to its "health." In Rohmer's film *The Marquise of O,* the lovers weep and the audience giggles.)

2.   Perhaps "weeping" is too crude; perhaps we must not refer all tears to one and the same signification; perhaps within the same lover there are several subjects who engage in neighboring but different modes of "weeping." Which is that "I" who has "tears in my eyes"? Which is that other self who, on a certain day, was "on the verge of tears"? Who am I who pours out "all the tears in my body"? or who sheds, upon waking, "a torrent of tears"? If I have so many ways of crying, it may be because, when I cry, I always address myself to someone, and because the recipient of my tears is not always the same: I adapt my ways of weeping to the kind of blackmail which, by my tears, I mean to exercise around me.

3.   By weeping, I want to impress someone, to bring pressure to bear upon someone ("Look what you have done to me"). It can be—as is commonly the case—the other whom one thus constrains to assume his commiseration or his insensibility quite openly; but it can also be oneself: I make myself cry, in order to prove to myself that my grief is not an illusion: tears are signs, not expressions. By my tears, I tell a story, I produce a myth of grief, and henceforth I adjust myself to it: I can live with it, because, by weeping, I give myself an emphatic interlocutor who receives the "truest" of messages, that of my body, not that of my speech: "Words, what are they? One tear will say more than all of them."

Schubert

SCHUBERT: *"Lob der Tränen."*

Gossip

potin / gossip

Pain suffered by the amorous subject when he finds
that the loved being is the subject of "gossip" and
hears that being discussed promiscuously.

Symposium

1.　　On the road from Phalerum, a bored traveler
catches sight of another man walking ahead of him,
catches up and asks him to tell about the banquet given by
Agathon. Such is the genesis of the theory of love: an
accident, boredom, a desire to talk, or, if you will, a gossip
lasting a little over a mile. Aristodemus has been to the
famous banquet; he has described it to Apollodorus, who,
on the road from Phalerum, tells the story of Glaucon (a
man, it is said, without any philosophic culture) and
thereby, by the book's mediation, tells it to us, who are
still discussing it. The *Symposium* is therefore not only a
"conversation" (we are discussing a question) but also a
gossip (we are speaking together about others).

This work derives, then, from two different linguistic
series, generally repressed—since official linguistics concerns itself only with the message. The first series would
postulate that no question (*quaestio*) can be put without
the texture of an interlocution; to speak of love, the guests
not only speak together, *from image to image, from place
to place* (in the *Symposium*, the arrangement of the

Symposium

SYMPOSIUM: Beginning.
SYMPOSIUM: Agathon: "Come here, O Socrates, take the couch next
to mine, so that I might benefit by the wise thoughts that have struck
you out there on the porch." And Alcibiades's entrance.

couches has a great importance), but further imply in his general discourse the amorous links which bind them (or which they imagine bind the others): such would be the linguistics of "conversation." The second series would say that to speak is always to say something about someone; in speaking about the banquet, about Love, it is about Socrates, about Alcibiades, and about their friends that Glaucon and Apollodorus are talking: the "subject" comes to light by gossip. An active philology (that of the forces of language) would therefore include two necessary linguistic series: that of interlocution (speaking to another) and that of delocution (speaking about someone).

2.   Werther has not yet made Charlotte's acquaintance; but in the carriage taking him to the ball (which is to pass Charlotte on the way), a friend—the voice of Gossip—discusses for Werther's benefit the woman whose image will in a few seconds so delight him: she is already engaged, he must not fall in love with her, etc. Thus gossip summarizes and heralds the story to come. Gossip is the voice of truth (Werther will fall in love with an object belonging to another), and this voice is magical: the friend is a wicked fairy who, under cover of admonishment, predicts and enforces.

Werther

When the friend speaks, her discourse is insensitive (a fairy has no pity): the gossip is light, cold, it thereby assumes the status of a kind of objectivity; its voice, in short, seems to double the voice of knowledge (*scientia*). These two voices are reductive. When knowledge, when science speaks, I sometimes come to the point of hearing its discourse as the sound of a gossip which describes and disparages lightly, coldly, and objectively what I love: which speaks of what I love *according to truth*.

3.   Gossip reduces the other to *he/she,* and this reduction is intolerable to me. For me the other is neither *he* nor *she;* the other has only a name of his own, and her own name. The third-person pronoun is a wicked pronoun: it is the pronoun of the non-person, it absents, it annuls. When I realize that common discourse takes possession of my other and restores that other to me in the bloodless form of a universal substitute, applied to all the things which are not here, it is as if I saw my other dead, reduced, shelved in an urn upon the wall of the great mausoleum of language. For me, the other cannot be a *referent:* you are never anything but you, I do not want the Other to speak of you.

Why?

pourquoi / why

Even as he obsessively asks himself why he is not
loved, the amorous subject lives in the belief that
the loved object does love him but does not tell
him so.

1.   There exists a "higher value" for me: my love. I
never say to myself: "What's the use?" I am not nihilistic.

Nietzsche I do not ask myself the question of ends. Never a "why"
in my monotonous discourse, except for one, always the
same: *But why is it that you don't love me?* How can one
not love this *me* whom love renders perfect (who gives so
much, who confers happiness, etc.)? A question whose
insistence survives the amorous episode: "Why didn't you
love me?"; or again: *O sprich, mein herzallerliebstes*

Heine *Lieb, warum verliessest du mich?*—O tell, love of my
heart, why have you abandoned me?

2.   Soon (or simultaneously) the question is no longer
"Why don't you love me?" but "Why do you only love me
a little?" How do you manage to love *a little?* What does
that mean, loving "a little"? I live under the regime of *too
much* or *not enough;* greedy for coincidence as I am,
everything which is not total seems parsimonious; what I
want is to occupy a site *from which quantities are no*

NIETZSCHE: "What does nihilism signify? *That the higher values are
losing their value.* The ends are lacking, there is no answer to this question 'What's the use?' "
HEINE: *"Lyrisches Intermezzo."*

longer perceived, and from which all accounts are banished.

Or again—for I am a nominalist: Why don't you *tell me* that you love me?

Freud

3.   The truth of the matter is that—by an exorbitant paradox—I never stop believing that I am loved. I hallucinate what I desire. Each wound proceeds less from a doubt than from a betrayal: for only the one who loves can betray, only the one who believes himself loved can be jealous: that the other, episodically, should fail in his being, which is to love me—that is the origin of all my woes. A delirium, however, does not exist unless one wakens from it (there are only retrospective deliriums): one day, I realize what has happened to me: I thought I was suffering from not being loved, and yet it is because I thought I was loved that I was suffering; I lived in the complication of supposing myself simultaneously loved and abandoned. Anyone hearing my intimate language would have had to exclaim, as of a difficult child: *But after all, what does he want?*

(*I love you* becomes *you love me.* One day, X receives some orchids, anonymously: he immediately hallucinates their source: they could only come from the person who loves him; and the person who loves him could only be the person he loves. It is only after a long period of investigation that he manages to dissociate the two inferences: the person who loves him is not necessarily the person he loves.)

FREUD: "We must take into account the fact that the hallucinatory psychosis of desire not only . . . brings concealed or repressed desires to consciousness but, further, represents them in all good faith as realized."

Ravishment

ravissement / ravishment

The supposedly initial episode (though it may be
reconstructed after the fact) during which the
amorous subject is "ravished" (captured and
enchanted) by the image of the loved object
(popular name: *love at first sight;* scholarly name:
enamoration).

Djedidi

1.   Language (vocabulary) has long since posited the
equivalence of love and war: in both cases, it is a matter
of *conquering, ravishing, capturing,* etc. Each time a subject "falls" in love, he revives a fragment of the archaic
time when men were supposed to carry off women (in
order to ensure exogamy): every lover who falls in love at
first sight has something of a Sabine Woman (or of some
other celebrated victim of ravishment).

However, there is an odd turnabout here: in the ancient
myth, the ravisher is active, he wants to seize his prey, he
is the subject of the rape (of which the object is a Woman,
as we know, invariably passive); in the modern myth
(that of love-as-passion), the contrary is the case: the
ravisher wants nothing, does nothing; he is motionless (as
any image), and it is the ravished object who is the real
subject of the rape; the *object* of capture becomes the
subject of love; and the *subject* of the conquest moves into
the class of loved *object*. (There nonetheless remains a
public vestige of the archaic model: the lover—the one

DJEDIDI, *La Poésie amoureuse des Arabes:* in Arabic, for instance, *fitna*
refers to both material (or ideological) warfare and the enterprise of
sexual seduction.

who has been ravished—is always implicitly feminized.)
This singular reversal may perhaps proceed from the fact
that for us the "subject" (since Christianity) is *the one
who suffers:* where there is a wound, there is a subject: *die
Wunde! die Wunde!* says Parsifal, thereby becoming

Parsifal

"himself"; and the deeper the wound, at the body's center
(at the "heart"), the more the subject becomes a subject:
for the subject is *intimacy* ("The wound . . . is of a
frightful intimacy"). Such is love's wound: a radical
chasm (at the "roots" of being), which cannot be closed,

Ruysbroeck

and out of which the subject drains, constituting himself as
a subject in this very draining. It would suffice to imagine
our Sabine Woman wounded to make her into the *subject*
of a love story.

2.   Love at first sight is a hypnosis: I am fascinated
by an image: at first shaken, electrified, stunned, "para-
lyzed" as Menon was by Socrates, the model of loved
objects, of captivating images, or again converted by an
apparition, nothing distinguishing the path of enamoration
from the Road to Damascus; subsequently ensnared, held
fast, immobilized, nose stuck to the image (the mirror).
In that moment when the other's image comes to ravish
me for the first time, I am nothing more than the Jesuit
Athanasius Kirchner's wonderful Hen: feet tied, the hen

Athanasius
Kirchner

went to sleep with her eyes fixed on the chalk line, which
was traced not far from her beak; when she was untied,
she remained motionless, fascinated, "submitting to her
vanquisher," as the Jesuit says (1646); yet, to waken her
from her enchantment, to break off the violence of her

RUYSBROECK: "The marrow of the bones wherein the roots of life reside
is the center of the wound . . . The gaping thing which is deep within
man does not readily close."
ATHANASIUS KIRCHNER: *Experimentum mirabile de imaginatione gal-
linae.*

Image-repertoire (*vehemens animalis imaginatio*), it was enough to tap her on the wing; she shook herself and began pecking in the dust again.

3.　　　　The hypnotic episode, it is said, is ordinarily preceded by a twilight state: the subject is in a sense empty, available, offered unwittingly to the rape which will surprise him. In the same way Werther describes at some length the trivial life he leads at Wahlheim before meeting Charlotte: no mundanity, no leisure, only reading Homer, a kind of blank and prosaic daily round, lulling him (he has nothing but pease porridge). This "wondrous serenity" is merely a waiting—a desire: I never fall in love unless I have wanted to; the emptiness I produce in myself (and on which, like Werther, quite innocently, I pride myself) is nothing but that interval, longer or shorter, when I glance around me, without seeming to, looking for *who to love*. Of course love requires a release switch, just as in the case of animal rape; the bait is occasional, but the structure is profound, regular, just as the mating season is seasonal. Yet the myth of "love at first sight" is so powerful (something that falls over me, without my expecting it, without my wanting it, without my taking the least part in it) that we are astonished if we hear of someone's *deciding* to fall in love: for example, Amadour seeing Florida at the court of the Viceroy of Catalonia: "After having gazed at her a long while, *he determined upon loving her*": *se délibéra*. Indeed, shall I deliberate if I must go mad (is love, then, that madness *I want?*)?

Freud

Werther

Heptameron

4.　　　　In the animal world, the release switch of the sexual mechanism is not a specific individual but only a form, a bright-colored fetish (which is how the Image-repertoire starts up). In the fascinating image, what impresses me (like a sensitized paper) is not the accumulation of its details but this or that inflection. What suddenly manages to touch me (ravish me) in the other is the voice, the line of the shoulders, the slenderness of the silhouette, the warmth of the hand, the curve of a smile, etc. Whereupon, what does the aesthetic of the image matter? Something accommodates itself exactly to my desire (about which I know nothing); I shall therefore make no concessions to style. Sometimes it is the other's conformity to a great cultural model which enthralls me (I imagine I see the other painted by an artist of the past); sometimes, on the contrary, it is a certain insolence of the apparition which will open the wound: I can fall in love with a slightly vulgar attitude (assumed out of provocation): there are

Flaubert

subtle, evanescent trivialities which swiftly pass over the other's body: a brief (but excessive) way of parting the fingers, of spreading the legs, of moving the fleshy part of the lips in eating, of going about some very prosaic occupation, of making one's body utterly idiotic for an instant, to keep oneself in countenance (what is fascinating

etymology

about the other's "triviality" is just this, perhaps: that for a very brief interval I surprise in the other, detached from the rest of his person, something like a gesture of prostitution). The feature which touches me refers to a fragment of behavior, to the fugitive moment of an attitude, a posture, in short to a *scheme* (σχῆμα, *schema,* is the body in movement, in situation, in life).

FLAUBERT: "And it seems that you are here, when I read love stories in books. —Everything that is taxed with being exaggerated, you have made me feel, Frédéric said. I understand how Werther could behave that way about Charlotte's bread-and-butter" (*Sentimental Educ...*
ETYMOLOGY: *Trivialis:* to be found at every crossroads (*trivi...*

5.   Stepping out of the carriage, Werther sees Charlotte for the first time (and falls in love with her), framed by the door of her house (cutting bread-and-butter for the children: a famous scene, often discussed): the first thing **Lacan** we love is *a scene.* For love at first sight requires the very sign of its suddenness (what makes me irresponsible, subject to fatality, swept away, ravished): and of all the arrangements of objects, it is the scene which seems to be seen best for the first time: a curtain parts: what had not yet ever been seen is discovered in its entirety, and then devoured by the eyes: what is immediate stands for what is fulfilled: I am initiated: the scene *consecrates* the object I am going to love. F ←

Anything is likely to ravish me which can reach me through a ring, a rip, a rent: "The first time I saw X through a car window: the window shifted, like a lens searching out *who to love* in the crowd; and then—immobilized by some *accuracy* of my desire?—I focused on that apparition whom I was henceforth to follow for months; but the other, as if he sought to resist this fresco in which he was lost as a subject, whenever he was subsequently to appear in my field of vision (walking into the café where I was waiting for him, for example) did so with every precaution, *a minimo,* impregnating his body with discretion and a kind of indifference, delaying his recognition of me, etc.: in short, trying to keep himself out of the picture."

always visual? It can be aural, the frame can I can fall in love with *a sentence spoken to* only because it says something which man- desire, but because of its syntactical turn will inhabit me *like a memory.*

Freud

6.   When Werther "discovers" Charlotte (when the curtain parts and the scene appears), Charlotte is cutting bread-and-butter. What Hanold falls in love with is a woman walking (*Gradiva:* the one who comes toward him), and furthermore glimpsed within the frame of a bas-relief. What fascinates, what ravishes me is the image of a body *in situation*. What excites me is an outline in action, *which pays no attention to me:* Grusha, the young servant, makes a powerful impression on the Wolf-man: she is on her knees, scrubbing the floor. For the posture of action, of labor, guarantees, in a way, *the innocence of the image:* the more the other grants me signs of his occupation, of his indifference, of my absence, the surer I am of surprising him, as if, in order to fall in love, I had to perform the ancestral formality of rape, i.e., surprise (I surprise the other and thereby he surprises me: I did not expect to surprise him).

7.   There is a deception in amorous time (this deception is called: the love story). I believe (along with everyone else) that the amorous phenomenon is an "episode" endowed with a beginning (love at first sight) and an end (suicide, abandonment, disaffection, withdrawal, monastery, travel, etc.). Yet the initial scene during which I was ravished is merely reconstituted: it is *after the fact*. I reconstruct a traumatic image which I experience in the present but which I conjugate (which I speak) in the past:

Racine

> *Je le vis, je rougis, je pâlis à sa vue.*
> *Un trouble s'éleva dans mon âme éperdue.*
> I saw him, blushed, turned pale when our eyes met.
> Confusion seized my bewildered soul.

FREUD: *The Wolf-man.*
RACINE: *Phèdre.*

Love at first sight is always spoken in the past tense: it might be called an *anterior immediacy*. The image is perfectly adapted to this temporal deception: distinct, abrupt, framed, it is already (again, always) a memory (the nature of the photograph is not to represent but to memorialize): when I "review" the scene of the rape, I retrospectively create a stroke of luck: this scene has all the magnificence of an accident: I cannot get over having had this good fortune: to meet what matches my desire; or to have taken this huge risk: instantly to submit to an unknown image (and the entire reconstructed scene functions like the sumptuous montage of an ignorance).

J.-L.B.

J.-L.B.: Conversation.

Regretted?

regretté / regretted

Imagining himself dead, the amorous subject sees
the loved being's life continue as if nothing had
happened.

Werther

1.   Werther overhears Lotte and one of her friends
gossiping; they are talking quite indifferently about a dying
man: "And yet . . . if you were to die, if you vanished
out of their lives? . . . Would your friends even notice?
How deeply would they feel the loss? How long would
your disappearance affect their destiny? . . ."

Not that I imagine myself dying without leaving regrets
behind: the obituary is determined: rather that through
the mourning itself, which I do not deny, I *see* the lives of
others continuing, without change; I see them persevering
in their occupations, their pastimes, their problems, fre-
quenting the same places, the same friends; nothing would
change in the train of their existence. Out of love, the
delirious assumption of Dependence (I have an *absolute*
need of the other), is generated, quite cruelly, the adverse
position: no one has any real need of me.

J.-L.B.

(Only the Mother can regret: to be depressed, it is said, is
to resemble the Mother as I imagine her regretting me
eternally: a dead, motionless image out of the *nekuia;* but
the others are not the Mother: for them, mourning; for
me, depression.)

J.-L.B.: Conversation.

2.   What increases Werther's panic is that the dying man (in whom he projects himself) is being *gossiped* about: Charlotte and her friends are "silly women" speaking frivolously about death. I envision myself nibbled up by others' words, dissolved in the ether of Gossip. And the Gossip will continue without my constituting any further part of it, no longer its object: a linguistic energy, trivial and tireless, will triumph over my very memory.

"How blue
the sky was"

rencontre / encounter

The figure refers to the happy interval immediately
following the first ravishment, before the
difficulties of the amorous relationship begin.

1.　　Though the lover's discourse is no more than a
dust of figures stirring according to an unpredictable
order, like a fly buzzing in a room, I can assign to love, at
least retrospectively, according to my Image-repertoire, a
settled course: it is by means of this *historical* hallucination that I sometimes make love into a romance, an adventure. This would appear to assume three stages (or
three acts): first comes the instantaneous capture (I am
ravished by an image); then a series of encounters (dates,
telephone calls, letters, brief trips), during which I ecstati-
cally "explore" the perfection of the loved being, i.e., the
unhoped-for correspondence between an object and my
desire: this is the sweetness of the beginning, the interval
proper to the idyll. This happy period acquires its identity
(its limits) from its opposition (at least in memory) to
the "sequel": the "sequel" is the long train of sufferings,
wounds, anxieties, distresses, resentments, despairs, em-

Ronsard

RONSARD: *"Quand je fus pris au doux commencement
D'une douceur si doucettement douce . . ."*

When I was caught up in the sweet beginning
Of a sweetness so deliciously sweet . . . (*"Doux fut le trait"*)

barrassments, and deceptions to which I fall prey, ceaselessly living under the threat of a downfall which would envelop at once the other, myself, and the glamorous encounter that first revealed us to each other.

2.   Some lovers do not commit suicide: it is possible for me to emerge from that "tunnel" which follows the amorous encounter. I see daylight again, either because I manage to grant unhappy love a dialectical outcome (retaining the love but getting rid of the hypnosis) or because I abandon that love altogether and set out again, trying to reiterate, with others, the encounter whose dazzlement remains with me: for it is of the order of the "first pleasure" and I cannot rest until it recurs: I affirm the affirmation, I begin again, without repeating.

(The encounter is radiant; later on, in memory, the subject will telescope into one the three moments of the amorous trajectory; he will speak of "love's dazzling tunnel.")

3.   In the encounter, I marvel that I have found someone who, by successive touches, each one successful, unfailing, completes the painting of my hallucination; I am like a gambler whose luck cannot fail, so that his hand unfailingly lands on the little piece which immediately completes the puzzle of his desire. This is a gradual discovery (and a kind of verification) of affinities, complicities, and intimacies which I shall (I imagine) eternally sustain with the other, who is thereby becoming "my other": I am totally given over to this discovery (I

199

tremble within it), to the point where any intense curiosity for someone encountered is more or less equivalent to love (it is certainly love which the young Moraïte feels for the traveler Chateaubriand, greedily watching his slightest gesture and following him until his departure). At every moment of the encounter, I discover in the other another myself: *You like this? So do I! You don't like that? Neither do I!* When Buvard and Pécuchet meet for the first time, they marvel over the catalogue of their shared tastes: the scene, beyond all doubt, is a love scene. The Encounter casts upon the (already ravished) amorous subject the dazzlement of a supernatural stroke of luck: love belongs to the (Dionysiac) order of the Cast of the dice.

Chateau-briand

Buvard and Pécuchet

(Neither knows the other yet. Hence they must tell each other: "This is what I am." This is narrative bliss, the kind which both fulfills and delays knowledge, in a word, *restarts* it. In the amorous encounter, I keep rebounding— I am *light*.)

R.H.

CHATEAUBRIAND: *Travels in Egypt, Palestine, Greece and Barbary.*
R.H.: Conversation.

Reverberation

retentissement / reverberation

Fundamental mode of amorous subjectivity: **a** word, an image reverberates painfully in the subject's affective consciousness.

1.   What echoes in me is what I learn with my body: something sharp and tenuous suddenly wakens this body, which, meanwhile, had languished in the rational knowledge of a general situation: the word, the image, the thought function like a whiplash. My inward body begins vibrating as though shaken by trumpets answering each other, drowning each other out: the incitation leaves its trace, the trace widens and everything is (more or less rapidly) ravaged. In the lover's Image-repertoire, nothing distinguishes the most trivial provocation from an authentically consequent phenomenon; time is jerked forward (catastrophic predictions flood to my mind) and back (I remember certain "precedents" with terror): starting from a negligible trifle, a whole discourse of memory and death rises up and sweeps me away: this is the kingdom of memory, weapon of reverberation—of what Nietzsche called *ressentiment*.

(Reverberation comes from Diderot's "unforeseen incident which . . . suddenly alters the state of the characters": it is a *coup de théâtre*, the "favorable moment" of a painting: pathetic scene of the ravaged, prostrated subject.)

2.   The space of reverberation is the body—that imaginary body, so "coherent" (coalescent) that I can experience it only in the form of a generalized pang. This pang (analogous to a blush which reddens the face, with shame or emotion) is a sudden panic. In the usual kind of panic—the stage fright which precedes some sort of performance—I see myself in the future in a condition of failure, imposture, scandal. In amorous panic, I am afraid of my own destruction, which I suddenly glimpse, inevitable, clearly formed, in the flash of a word, an image.

Diderot

3.   When his sentences ran dry, Flaubert flung himself on his divan: he called this his "marinade." If the thing reverberates too powerfully, it makes such a din in my body that I must halt any occupation; I stretch out on my bed and give in without a struggle to the "inner storm"; contrary to the Zen monk who empties himself of his images, I let myself be filled by them, I indulge their bitterness to the full. Depression has its own—encoded— *gestus,* then, and doubtless that is what limits it; for it suffices that at a given moment I can substitute another (even blank) gesture for this one (getting up, going to my desk, without necessarily working there, right away), to make the reverberation die down, giving way to no more than *ennui.* The bed (by day) is the site of the Image-repertoire; the desk is once again, and whatever one does there, reality.

Ruysbroeck

DIDEROT: "The word is not the thing, but a flash in whose light we perceive the thing."

4.　　X tells me about a disagreeable rumor which concerns me. This incident reverberates within me in two ways: on the one hand, I receive the object of the message at point-blank range, outraged by its imposture, eager to deny it, etc.; on the other hand, I am perfectly conscious of the little impulse of aggression which has impelled X —without his being exactly aware of it himself—to pass on this wounding intelligence. Traditional linguistics would analyze only the message: conversely, active Philology would try especially to interpret, to evaluate the (here, reactive) force which directs (or attracts) it. Now, what is it that I do? I conjugate the two linguistic series, amplify them by each other: I establish myself, however painfully, in the very substance of the message (i.e., the content of the rumor), while I bitterly and mistrustfully scrutinize the force which warrants it: I lose on both counts, wounded on all sides. This is reverberation: the zealous practice of a perfect reception: contrary to the analyst (and with reason), far from "floating" while the other speaks, I listen *completely,* in a state of total consciousness: I cannot keep from hearing everything, and it is the purity of this reception which is painful to me: who can tolerate without pain a meaning that is complex and yet purified of any "noise" or interference? Reverberation makes reception into an intelligible din, and the lover into a monstrous receiver, reduced to an enormous auditive organ—as if listening itself were to become a state of utterance: in me, it is the ear which speaks.

Aubade

réveil / waking

Various modes by which the amorous subject finds upon waking that he is once again besieged by the anxieties of his passion.

Werther

s.s.

Werther

1.   Werther speaks of his exhaustion ("Let me suffer to the end: for all my exhaustion, I still have strength enough for that"). Amorous anxiety involves an expenditure which tires the body as harshly as any physical labor. "I suffered so much," someone said, "I struggled so hard all day with the image of the loved being, that I always slept very well at night." And Werther, shortly before committing suicide, goes to bed and sleeps very soundly.

Stendhal

2.   Modes of waking: sad, wracked (with tenderness), affectless, innocent, panic-stricken (Octave comes to, after fainting: "All of a sudden his miseries were clear in his mind: one does not die of pain, or he was a dead man at that moment").

s.s.: Reported by S.S.
STENDHAL: *Armance.*

Making Scenes

scène / scene

The figure comprehends every "scene" (in the household sense of the term) as an exchange of reciprocal contestations.

1.　When two subjects argue according to a set exchange of remarks and with a view to having the "last word," these two subjects are *already* married: for them the scene is an exercise of a right, the practice of a language of which they are co-owners; *each one in his turn,* says the scene, which means: *never you without me,* and reciprocally. This is the meaning of what is euphemistically called *dialogue:* not to listen to each other, but to submit in common to an egalitarian principle of the distribution of language goods. The partners know that the confrontation in which they are engaged, and which will not separate them, is as inconsequential as a perverse form of pleasure (the scene is a way of taking pleasure without the risk of having children).

With the first scene, language begins its long career as an agitated, useless thing. It is dialogue (the joust of two actors) which corrupted Tragedy, even before Socrates appeared on the scene. Monologue is thereby pushed back to the very limits of humanity: in archaic tragedy, in cer-

Nietzsche

NIETZSCHE: "There already had existed something analogous in the exchange of remarks between the hero and the choryphaeus, but since the one was subordinate to the other, dialectical *combat* was impossible. But once two principal characters stood face to face, there was born, conforming to a profoundly Hellenic instinct, the battle of words and of arguments: amorous dialogue [what we mean by *the scene*] was unknown to Greek tragedy."

tain forms of schizophrenia, in amorous soliloquy (at least as long as I "keep" my delirium and do not yield to the desire to draw the other into a set contestation of language). It is as if the proto-actor, the madman, and the lover refused to posit themselves as hero of speech and to submit to adult language, the social language to which they are prompted by the wicked Eris: the language of universal neurosis.

2.   *Werther* is pure discourse of the amorous subject: the (idyllic, anguished) monologue is broken only once, at the end, just before the suicide: Werther pays a visit to Charlotte, who asks him not to come and see her again before Christmas day, thereby signifying to him that he must visit less frequently and that henceforth his passion will no longer be "received": there follows a scene. The scene starts with a disagreement: Charlotte is embarrassed, Werther is excited, and Charlotte's embarrassment excites Werther all the more: thus the scene has only one subject, divided by a differential of energy (the scene is *electric*). So that this disequilibrium can *catch* (like a motor), so that the scene can get into its proper gear, there must be a bait or decoy which each of the two partners tries to draw into his own camp; this bait is usually a fact (which one affirms and the other denies) or a decision (which one imposes and the other rejects: in *Werther,* to visit less frequently). Agreement is logically impossible insofar as what is being argued is not the fact or the decision, i.e., something which is outside language, but only precedes it: the scene has no object or at least very soon loses its object: it is that language whose object is lost. It is characteristic of the individual remarks in a scene to have no demonstrative, persuasive end, but only

an origin, and this origin is never anything but immediate: in the scene, I cling to what has just been said. The (divided and yet mutual) subject of the scene is uttered in distichs: this is stichomythia, the archaic model of all the scenes in the world (when we are in a "state of scene," we speak in "rows" of words). Yet, whatever the regularity of this mechanism, the initial differential must be discoverable in each distich: thus Charlotte always turns her argument toward general propositions ("It's because it is impossible that you desire me at all"), and Werther always brings his argument back to contingence, god of amorous injury ("Your decision must have been made by Albert"). Each argument (each verse of the distich) is chosen so that it will be symmetrical and, so to speak, equal to its brother, and yet augmented with an additional protest; in short, with a *higher bid*. This bid is never anything but Narcissus's cry: *Me! And me! What about me!*

etymology

3.   The scene is like the Sentence: structurally, there is no obligation for it to stop; no internal constraint exhausts it, because, as in the Sentence, once the core is given (the fact, the decision), the expansions are infinitely renewable. Only some circumstance external to its structure can interrupt the scene: the exhaustion of the two partners (that of only one would not suffice), the arrival of a third party (in *Werther,* it is Albert), or else the sudden substitution of desire for aggression. Unless these accidents are employed, no partner has the power to check a scene. What means might I have? Silence? It would merely quicken the *will to have* the scene; I am therefore obliged to answer in order to soothe, to erase. Reasoning? None is of such pure metal as to leave the other partner

ETYMOLOGY: στίχος (*stichos*): row, file.

without something to say. Analysis of the scene itself? To shift from the scene to the metascene merely means opening another scene. Flight? This is the sign of a defection already achieved: the couple is *already* undone: like love, the scene is always reciprocal. Hence, the scene is interminable, like language itself: it is language itself, taken in its infinity, that "perpetual adoration" which brings matters about in such a way that since man has existed, *he has not stopped talking.*

(The good thing about X was that he never exploited the sentence that was given to him; by a kind of rare *askesis, he did not take advantage of language.*)

4.   No scene has a meaning, no scene moves toward an enlightenment or a transformation. The scene is neither practical nor dialectical; it is a luxury—and idle: as inconsequential as a perverse orgasm: it does not leave a mark, it does not sully. Paradox: in Sade, violence, too, does not leave a mark; the body is instantaneously restored—for new expenditures: endlessly lacerated, tainted, crushed, Justine is always fresh, whole, rested; the same is true of the scene's partners: they are reborn from the past scene as if nothing had occurred. By the very insignificance of its tumult, the scene recalls the Roman style of vomiting: I tickle my uvula (I rouse myself to contestation), I vomit (a flood of wounding arguments), and then, quite calmly, I begin eating again.

Sade

5.   Insignificant as it is, the scene nonetheless struggles against insignificance. Each partner of a scene dreams of having the *last word*. To speak last, "to conclude," is to

assign a destiny to everything that has been said, is to master, to possess, to absolve, to bludgeon meaning; in the space of speech, the one who comes last occupies a sovereign position, held, according to an established privilege, by professors, presidents, judges, confessors: every language combat (the *machia* of the Sophists, the *disputatio* of the Scholastics) seeks to gain possession of this position; by the last word, I will disorganize, "liquidate" the adversary, inflicting upon him a (narcissistically) mortal wound, cornering him in silence, castrating him of all speech. The scene passes with a view to this triumph: there is no question whatever that each remark should contribute to the victory of a truth, gradually constructing this truth, but only that the *last* remark be the right one: it is the last throw of the dice which counts. The scene bears no resemblance to a chess game, but rather to a game of hunt-the-slipper: yet here the game is inverted, for the victory goes to the one who manages to keep the slipper in his hand at the very moment the game stops: the slipper changes hands throughout the scene, and the victory goes to the player who captures that little creature whose possession assures omnipotence: the last word.

Werther

In *Werther,* the scene is crowned with a blackmail: "Grant me only a little peace and everything will be settled," Werther says to Charlotte in a plaintive yet threatening tone: which is to say: "You will soon be rid of me": a proposition marked with a certain voluptuous quality, for it is in fact hallucinated as a *last word*. In order that the subject of the scene be furnished with a truly peremptory last word, it requires no less than suicide: by the announcement of suicide, Werther immediately becomes *the stronger of the two:* whereby we see once again that only death can interrupt the Sentence, the Scene.

Kierkegaard

What is a hero? The one who has the last word. Can we think of a hero who does not speak before dying? To renounce the last word (to refuse to have a scene) derives, then, from an anti-heroic morality: that of Abraham: to the end of the sacrifice demanded of him, he does not speak. Or else, as a more subversive because less theatrical riposte (silence is always sufficient theater), the last word may be replaced by an incongruous pirouette: this is what the Zen master did who, for his only answer to the solemn question "What is Buddha?," took off his sandal, put it on his head, and walked away: impeccable dissolution of the last word, mastery of non-mastery.

KIERKEGAARD: *Fear and Trembling.*

"No clergyman attended"

seul / alone

The figure refers, not to what the human solitude of the amorous subject may be, but to his "philosophical" solitude, love-as-passion being accounted for today by no major system of thought (of discourse).

1.　　What do we call that subject who persists in an "error" against and counter to everyone, as if he had before himself all eternity in which to be "mistaken"? We call him a *relapse*. Whether it be from one lover to the next or within one and the same love, I keep "falling back" into an interior doctrine which no one shares with me. When Werther's body is taken by night to a corner of the cemetery, near two lindens (the tree whose simple odor is that of memory and sleep), "no clergyman attended" (the novel's last sentence). Religion condemns in Werther not only the suicide but also, perhaps, the lover, the utopian, the class heretic, the man who is "ligatured" to no one but himself.

Werther

etymology

2.　　In the *Symposium,* Eryximachus notes with some irony that he has read somewhere a panegyric of salt, but nothing on Eros, and it is because Eros is censured as a subject of conversation that the little society of the

Symposium

ETYMOLOGY: *Religare,* to tie together, to ligature.

Symposium decides to make this the subject of its round table: rather like today's intellectuals reluctantly agreeing to discuss, precisely, Love and not politics, (amorous) Desire and not (social) Need. The eccentricity of the conversation derives from the fact that this conversation is systematic: what the guests try to produce are not proved remarks, accounts of experiences, but a doctrine: for each of them, Eros is a system. Today, however, there is no system of love: and the several systems which surround the contemporary lover offer him no room (except for an extremely devaluated place): turn as he will toward one or another of the received languages, none answers him, except in order to turn him away from what he loves. Christian discourse, if it still exists, exhorts him to repress and to sublimate. Psychoanalytical discourse (which, at least, describes his state) commits him to give up his Image-repertoire as lost. As for Marxist discourse, it has nothing to say. If it should occur to me to knock at these doors in order to gain recognition *somewhere* (wherever it might be) for my "madness" (my "truth"), these doors close one after the other; and when they are all shut, there rises around me a wall of language which oppresses and repulses me—unless I *repent* and agree to "get rid of X."

("I have had that nightmare about a loved person who was sick in the street and begged the passers-by for help; but everyone refused him harshly, despite my own hysterical attempts to obtain medicine; the anguish of this loved person then became hysterical, for which I reproached him. I understood a little later that his person was myself —of course; who else is there to dream about?: I was appealing to all the passing languages (systems), rejected by them and pleading with all my might, *indecently*, for a philosophy which might 'understand' me—might 'shelter' me.")

3.   The lover's solitude is not a solitude of person (love confides, speaks, tells itself), it is a solitude of system: I am alone in making a system out of it (perhaps because I am ceaselessly flung back on the solipsism of my discourse). A difficult paradox: I can be understood by everyone (love comes from books, its dialect is a common one), but I can be heard (received "prophetically") only by subjects who have *exactly and right now* the same language I have. Lovers, Alcibiades says, are like those a viper has bitten: "They are unwilling, it is said, to speak of their misfortune to anyone except those who have been victims of it as well, as being the only ones in a position to conceive and to excuse all they have dared to say and do in the throes of their pain": paltry troupe of "Starved souls," the Suicides for love (how many times will not one and the same lover commit suicide?), to whom no great language (save, fragmentarily, that of the passé Novel) lends its voice.

Symposium

Ruysbroeck

4.   Like the early mystic, scarcely tolerated by the ecclesiastical society in which he lived, as an amorous subject I neither confront nor contest: quite simply, I have no dialogue: with the instruments of power, of thought, of knowledge, of action, etc.; I am not necessarily "depoliticized": my deviation consists in not being "excited." In return, society subjects me to a strange, public repression: no censure, no prohibition: I am merely suspended *a humanis,* far from human things, by a tacit decree of in-

significance: I belong to no repertoire, participate in no asylum.

5.   Why I am alone:

Tao

"Every man has his wealth,
I alone appear impoverished.
My mind is that of an ignorant man
because it is very slow.
Every man is clear-sighted,
I alone am in darkness.
Every man has a sharp wit,
I alone have a clouded mind
Which floats with the sea, blows with the wind.
Every man has his goal,
I alone have the dull mind of a peasant.
I alone am different from other men,
For I seek to suckle at my Mother's breast."

TAO: *Tao Te Ching.*

The Uncertainty
of Signs

signes / signs

Whether he seeks to prove his love, or to discover
if the other loves him, the amorous subject has no
system of sure signs at his disposal.

1.   I look for signs, but of what? What is the object of
my reading? Is it: am I loved (am I loved no longer, am I
still loved)? Is it my future that I am trying to read,
deciphering in what is inscribed the announcement of what
will happen to me, according to a method which combines
paleography and manticism? Isn't it rather, all things con-
sidered, that I remain suspended on this question, whose
answer I tirelessly seek in the other's face: *What am I
worth?*

Balzac

2.   The power of the Image-repertoire is immediate: I
do not look for the image, it comes to me, all of a sudden.
It is afterwards that I return to it and begin making the
good sign alternate, interminably, with the bad one:
"What do these abrupt words mean: you have all my
respect? Was anything ever colder? Is this a complete
return to the old intimacy? Or a polite way to cut short a
disagreeable explanation?" Like Stendhal's Octave, I
never know what is *normal;* lacking (as I well know) all

Stendhal

BALZAC: "She was learned and she knew that the amorous character has
its signs in what are taken for trifles. A knowledgeable woman can read
her future in a simple gesture, as Cuvier could say, seeing the fragment
of a paw: this belongs to an animal of such-and-such a size," etc.
(*The Secrets of the Princess of Cadignan*).
STENDHAL: *Armance.*

reason, I would prefer, in order to decide on an interpretation, to trust myself to common sense; but common sense affords me no more than contradictory evidence: "After all, it's not really normal to go out in the middle of the night and to come home four hours later!" "After all, it's only normal to go out and take a walk when you can't sleep," etc. A man who wants the truth is never answered save in strong, highly colored images, which nonetheless turn ambiguous, indecisive, once he tries to transform them into signs: as in any manticism, the consulting lover must make his own truth.

3.   Freud to his fiancée: "The only thing that makes me suffer is being in a situation where it is impossible for me to prove my love to you." And Gide: "Everything in her behavior seemed to say: Since he no longer loves me, nothing matters to me. Now, I still loved her, and in fact I had never loved her so much; but it was no longer possible for me to prove it to her. That was much the worst thing of all."

Freud

Gide

Signs are not proofs, since anyone can produce false or ambiguous signs. Hence one falls back, paradoxically, on the omnipotence of language: since nothing assures language, I will regard it as the sole and final assurance: *I shall no longer believe in interpretation*. I shall receive every word from my other as a sign of truth; and when I speak, I shall not doubt that he, too, receives what I say as the truth. Whence the importance of *declarations;* I want to keep wresting from the other the formula of his feeling, and I keep telling him, on my side, that I love him: nothing is left to suggestion, to divination: for a thing to be known, it must be spoken; but also, once it is spoken, even very provisionally, it is true.

FREUD: *Letters.*
GIDE: *Journal,* 1939.

"*E lucevan le stelle*"

souvenir / remembrance

Happy and/or tormenting remembrance of an
object, a gesture, a scene, linked to the loved being
and marked by the intrusion of the imperfect
tense into the grammar of the lover's discourse.

Werther

1.   "It is a glorious summer, and I often sit up in the
trees of Lotte's orchard and take down with a long pole
the pears from the highest branches. She stands below and
catches them when I lower the pole." Werther is telling his
story, and speaks in the present tense, but his scene already has the vocation of a remembrance; in an under-
tone, the imperfect tense murmurs behind this present.
One day, I shall recall the scene, I shall lose myself *in the
past*. The amorous scene, like the first ravishment, consists
only of *after-the-fact* manipulations: this is *anamnesis,*
which recovers only insignificant features in no way
dramatic, as if I remembered time itself and only time: it
is a fragrance without support, a texture of memory;
something like a pure expenditure, such as only the
Japanese haiku has been able to articulate, without
recuperating it in any destiny.

(To gather the figs from the high branches in the garden in
B., there was a long bamboo pole and a tin funnel stamped
with rosettes that was fastened to it: this childhood memory functions in the same way as an amorous one.)

Tosca

2.   "The stars were shining." Never again will this happiness return *just this way*. Anamnesis both fulfills and lacerates me.

Proust

The imperfect is the tense of fascination: it seems to be alive and yet it doesn't move: imperfect presence, imperfect death; neither oblivion nor resurrection; simply the exhausting lure of memory. From the start, greedy to play a role, scenes take their position in memory: often I feel this, I foresee this, at the very moment when these scenes are forming. —This theater of time is the very contrary of the search for lost time; for I remember pathetically, punctually, and not philosophically, discursively: I remember in order to be unhappy/happy—not in order to understand. I do not write, I do not shut myself up in order to write the enormous novel of time recaptured.

Ideas of Suicide

suicide / suicide

In the amorous realm, the desire for suicide is
frequent: a trifle provokes it.

1.   For the slightest injury, I want to commit suicide:
upon meditation, amorous suicide does figure as a motif.
The notion is a light one—an easy idea, a kind of rapid
algebra which my discourse requires at this particular
moment; I grant it no substantial consistency, nor do I
foresee the heavy décor, the trivial consequences of death:
I scarcely know *how* I am going to kill myself. It is a
phrase, only a sentence, which I darkly caress but from
which a trifle will distract me. "And the man who for three
quarters of an hour had just planned his own death stood
at this very moment on a chair to search his bookshelves
for the price list of the Saint-Gobain mirrors."

Stendhal

2.   Sometimes, in the brilliant light cast by some
trivial circumstance and swept away by the reverberations
the incident has provoked, I suddenly see myself caught in
the trap, immobilized in an impossible situation (site):
there are only two ways out (either . . . or) and they
are both barred: nothing to be said in either direction.
Then the idea of suicide saves me, for *I can speak it* (and
do not fail to do so): I am reborn and dye this idea with
the colors of life, either directing it aggressively against the
loved object (a familiar blackmail) or in fantasy uniting

STENDHAL: *Armance.*

Heine

myself with the loved object in death ("I shall lie down in the grave, pressed close against you").

3.   Upon discussion, the scientists conclude that animals do not commit suicide; at most, certain species— horses, dogs—have an impulse to self-mutilation. Yet it is apropos of horses that Werther intimates the *nobility* which marks every suicide: "I have been told that a noble

Werther

breed of horses, when overheated and hunted almost to death, will by instinct bite open a vein and so recover their breath. I often feel the same. I should like to open one of my veins and gain eternal freedom for myself."

Gide's silliness: "Just finished rereading *Werther,* not without irritation. I had forgotten how long it took him to die [which is not at all the case]. He keeps going on and

Gide

on, until you want to give him a push, right into the grave. Four or five times, what you had hoped was his last breath is followed by another even more ultimate one . . . the extended leave-takings exasperate me." Gide doesn't real-ize that in the novel of love, the hero is *real* (because he is created out of an absolutely projective substance in which every amorous subject collects himself), and that what he is looking for here is a man's death—is *my* death.

HEINE: *"Lyrisches Intermezzo."*
GIDE: *Journal,* 1940.

Thus

tel / thus

Endlessly required to define the loved object, and
suffering from the uncertainties of this definition,
the amorous subject dreams of a knowledge which
would let him take the other *as he is*, thus and no
other, exonerated from any adjective.

1.   Narrow-mindedness: as a matter of fact, I admit
nothing about the other, I understand nothing. Everything
about the other which doesn't concern me seems alien,
hostile; I then feel toward him a mixture of alarm and
severity: I fear and I reprove the loved being, once he no
longer "sticks" to his image. I am merely "liberal": a
doleful dogmatic, so to speak.

(Industrious, indefatigable, the language machine humming inside me—for it runs nicely—fabricates its chain of
adjectives: I cover the other with adjectives, I string out
his qualities, his *qualitas*.)

2.   Through these iridescent, versatile judgments, a
painful impression subsists: I see that the other perseveres
in himself; he is himself this perseverance, against which I
stumble. I realize with hysteria that I cannot *displace* him;
whatever I do, whatever I expend for him, he never
renounces his own system. I contradictorily experience the
other as a capricious divinity who keeps changing his
moods in my respect, *and* as a heavy, *inveterate* thing

etymology

(this thing will age just as it is, and that is what I suffer from). Or again, I see the other *in his limits.* Or finally, I question myself: Is there even a single point as to which the other might *surprise me?* Thus, curiously, the other's "freedom to be himself" I experience as a cowardly stubbornness. I see the other *thus*—I see the other's *thusness* —but in the realm of amorous sentiment this *thus* is painful to me because it separates us and because, once again, I refuse to recognize the division of our image, the other's alterity.

3.   This first *thus* is wrong because I leave on the blotter, as an internal point of corruption, an adjective: the other is *stubborn:* he still derives from *qualitas.* I must get rid of any impulse to draw up accounts; the other must become, in my eyes, pure of any attribution; the more I designate him, the less I shall utter him: I shall be like the *infans* who contents himself with a blank word to show something: Ta, Da, Tat (says Sanskrit). *Thus,* the lover

Zen

will say: *you are thus, thus and so, precisely thus.*

Designating you as *thus,* I enable you to escape the death of classification, I kidnap you from the Other, from language, I want you to be immortal. *As he is,* the loved being no longer receives any meaning, neither from myself nor from the system in which he is caught; he is no more than a text without context; I no longer need or desire to decipher him; he is in a sense the *supplement of his own site.* If he were only a site, I might well, someday, replace him, but I can substitute nothing for the supplement of his site, his *thus.*

(In restaurants, once the last service is over, the tables are set again for the next day: same white cloth, same silver-

ETYMOLOGY: *Inveterare,* to age, to grow old.

J.-L.B. ware, same salt and pepper shakers: this is the world of site, of replacement: no *thus*.)

4.   So I accede, fitfully, to a language without adjectives. I love the other, not according to his (accountable) qualities, but according to his existence; by a movement one might well call mystical, I love, not what he is, but *that he is*. The language in which the amorous subject then protests (against all the nimble languages of the world) is an *obtuse* language: every judgment is suspended, the terror of meaning is abolished. What I liquidate in this movement is the very category of merit: just as the mystic makes himself indifferent to sanctity (which would still be an attribute), so, acceding to the other's *thus*, I no longer oppose oblation to desire: it seems to me that I can make myself desire the other less and delight in him more.

(The worst enemy of *thus* is Gossip, corrupt manufacturer of adjectives. And what would best resemble the loved being *as he is, thus and so,* would be the Text, to which I can add no adjective: which I delight in without having to decipher it.)

Nietzsche 5.   Or again: is not *thus* the friend? He who can leave for a while without his image crumbling? "We were friends and have become estranged. But this was right, and we do not want to conceal and obscure it from ourselves as if we had reason to feel ashamed. We are two ships each of which has its goal and course; our paths may cross and we may celebrate a feast together, as we did—

J.-L.B.: Conversation.
NIETZSCHE: "Star Friendship," *The Gay Science*.

and then the good ships rested so quietly in one harbor and one sunshine that it may have looked as if they had reached their goal and as if they had one goal. But then the mighty force of our tasks drove us apart again into different seas and sunny zones, and perhaps we shall never see each other again; perhaps we shall meet again but fail to recognize each other: our exposure to different seas and suns has changed us."

Tenderness

tendresse / tenderness
Bliss, but also a disturbing evaluation of the loved
object's tender gestures, insofar as the subject
realizes that he is not their privileged recipient.

1.   There is not only need for tenderness, there is also
need to be tender for the other: we shut ourselves up in a
mutual kindness, we mother each other reciprocally; we
return to the root of all relations, where need and desire

Musil

join. The tender gesture says: ask me anything that can
put your body to sleep, but also do not forget that I desire
you—a little, lightly, without trying to seize anything right
away.

Sexual pleasure is not metonymic: once taken, it is cut
off: it was the Feast, always terminated and instituted only
by a temporary, supervised lifting of the prohibition. Tenderness, on the contrary, is nothing but an infinite, in-
satiable metonymy; the gesture, the episode of tenderness
(the delicious harmony of an evening) can only be interrupted with laceration: everything seems called into ques-

Zen

tion once again: return of rhythm—*vritti*—disappearance
of *nirvana*.

2.   If I receive the tender gesture within the field of
demand, I am fulfilled: is this gesture not a kind of

MUSIL: "Her brother's body pressed so tenderly, so sweetly against her,
that she felt she was resting within him even as he in her; nothing in her
stirred now, even her splendid desire" (*The Man without Qualities*, II).
ZEN: *Vritti*, for the Buddhist, is the series of waves, the cyclic process.
Vritti is painful, and only *nirvana* can put an end to it.

miraculous crystallization of presence? But if I receive it (and this can be simultaneous) within the field of desire, I am disturbed: tenderness, by rights, is not exclusive, hence I must admit that what I receive, others receive as well (sometimes I am even afforded the spectacle of this). Where you are tender, you speak your plural.

("L was stupefied to see A give the waitress in the Bavarian restaurant, while ordering his schnitzel, the same tender look, the same angelic expression that moved him so when these expressions were addressed to him.")

Union

union / union

Dream of total union with the loved being.

Musil

1. Naming of the total union: "the sole and simple pleasure" (Aristotle), "the joy without stain and without mixture, the perfection of dreams, the term of all hopes" (Ibn-Hazm), "the divine magnificence" (Novalis); it is undifferentiated and undivided repose. Or again, the fulfillment of ownership; I dream that we delight in each other according to an absolute appropriation; this is fruitful union, love's *fruition* (with its initial fricative and shifting vowels before the murmuring final syllable, the word increases the delight it speaks of by an oral pleasure; saying it, I enjoy this union *in my mouth*).

Ronsard

Lacan

2. *En sa moytié, ma moytié je recolle*—to her half, I rejoin my own half. I leave a (mediocre) film in which a character evokes Plato and the theory of the Hermaphrodites. Apparently, everyone knows the story of the two halves trying to join themselves back together (desire is to lack what one has—and to give what one does not have: a matter of supplements, not complements).

(I spend an afternoon trying to draw what Aristophanes'

MUSIL: "And in this repose, united and without separation, even without separation inside herself, until their intelligence seemed lost, their memory drained, their will useless, she stood up within this repose as before a sunrise and lost herself in it entirely, she and all her earthly particularities" (*The Man without Qualities*, II).
RONSARD: *Les Amours*, CXXVII.
LACAN: *Le Séminaire*, XI. And: "Psychoanalysis seeks the missing organ (the libido) and not the missing half." (A pity!)

hermaphrodite would look like: globular, with four hands, four legs, four ears, just one head, one neck. Are the halves back to back or face to face? Belly to belly, no doubt, since Apollo was to sew them up again here, drawing the skin together and creating the navel: yet their faces are facing away from each other, since Apollo was to turn them toward the side where he had divided them; and the genital organs are behind. I persist, but get nowhere, being a poor draughtsman or an even poorer utopianist. The hermaphrodite, or the androgyne, figure of that "ancient unity of which the desire and the pursuit constitute what we call love," is beyond my figuration; or at least all I could achieve is a monstrous, grotesque, improbable body. Out of dreams emerges a farce figure: thus, out of the mad couple is born the obscenity of the *household* (one cooks, for life, for the other).

Symposium

3.   Phaedrus seeks the perfect image of the couple: Orpheus and Eurydice? Not enough difference: Orpheus, weakened, was nothing but a woman, and the gods caused him to die at women's hands. Admetus and Alcestis? Better: the wife substitutes herself for the failing parents, she wrests the son from his name and gives him another: thus there always remains a man in the business. Yet the perfect couple is Achilles and Patroclus: not according to a homosexual *parti pris,* but because within the same sex the difference remains inscribed: Patroclus was the lover, Achilles the beloved. Thus—according to Nature, traditional wisdom, the myth—do not look for union (amphimixis) outside the division of roles, if not of the sexes: it is the couple's *reason.*

Freud

Eccentric (scandalous), the dream furnishes the contrary image. In the dual form I fantasize, I want there to be a

FREUD: Amphimixis is a mixture of the substances of two individuals.

point without an *elsewhere,* I sigh (not a very modern action) for a *centered* structure, balanced by the consistency of the Same: if *everything* is not in *two,* what's the use of struggling? I might as well return to the pursuit of the multiple. As for this *everything* I desire, it suffices for its fulfillment (the dream insists) that each of us be without sites: that we be able magically to substitute for each other: that the kingdom of *"one for the other"* come ("In going together, each will think for the other"), as if we were the vocables of a new, strange language, in which it would be quite licit to use one word for another. This union would be without limits, not by the scope of its expansion, but by the indifference of its permutations. (What do I care about a limited relation? It makes me suffer. Doubtless, if someone were to ask me: "How are things going with you and X?" I should reply: Right now I'm exploring our limits; ninny that I am, I make the advances, I circumscribe our common territory. But what I dream of is all the others in a single person; for if I united X, Y, and Z, by the line passing through all these presently starred points, I should form a perfect figure: my other would be born.)

Symposium

4.   Dream of total union: everyone says this dream is impossible, and yet it persists. I do not abandon it. "On the Athenian steles, instead of the heroicization of death, scenes of farewell in which one of the spouses takes leave of the other, hand in hand, at the end of a contract which only a third force can break, thus it is mourning which achieves its expression here . . . I am no longer myself without you." It is in *represented* mourning that we find the proof of my dream; I can believe in it, since it is mortal (the only impossible thing is immortality).

François
Wahl

SYMPOSIUM: Quotation from the *Iliad,* Book X.
FRANÇOIS WAHL: *"Chute."*

Truth

vérité / truth

Every episode of language refers to the "sensation
of truth" the amorous subject experiences in
thinking of his love, either because he believes he
is the only one to see the loved object "in its truth,"
or because he defines the specialty of his own
requirement as a truth concerning which he
cannot yield.

Werther

Freud

1.   The other is my good and my knowledge: only I
know him, only I make him exist in his truth. Whoever is
not me is ignorant of the other: "Sometimes I cannot
understand how another *can,* how he *dare* love her, since I
alone love her completely and devotedly, knowing only
her, and having nothing in the world but her!" Conversely,
the other establishes me in truth: it is only with the other
that I feel I am "myself." I know more about myself than
all those who simply do not know this about me: that I
am in love.

(Love is blind: the proverb is false. Love opens his eyes
wide, love produces clear-sightedness: "I have, about you,
of you, absolute knowledge." Report of the clerk to the
master: *You have every mastery of me, but I have every
knowledge of you.*)

2.   Always the same reversal: what the world takes
for "objective," I regard as factitious; and what the world

FREUD: "A man who doubts his own love can, or rather *must,* doubt
every less important thing" (quoted by Melanie Klein).

regards as madness, illusion, error, I take for truth. It is in the deepest part of the lure that the sensation of truth comes to rest. The lure sheds its décor, it becomes so pure, like a primary metal, that nothing can ever change it: it is indestructible. Werther has made up his mind to die: "I write you this without novelistic exaltation, quite calmly." Displacement: it is not the truth which is true, but the relation to the lure which becomes true. To be in the truth, it is enough to persist: a "lure" endlessly affirmed, against everything, becomes a truth. (And suppose there might be, ultimately, in love-as-passion, a fragment of real . . . truth.)

Werther

3.   The truth is what, being taken away, leaves nothing to be seen but death (as we say: life is no longer worth living). Thus with the name of the Golem: *Emeth* (Truth); take one letter away and he becomes *Meth* (he is dead). Or again: truth is what, in the fantasy of hallucination, must be delayed but not denied, betrayed: its irreducible portion, what I do not cease wanting to know once before dying (another formulation: "Then I shall die without having known . . ." etc.).

Jakob Grimm

(The lover botches his castration? Out of this failure, he persists in making a *value*.)

GRIMM: *Journal for Hermits:* "The Polish Jews make the figure of a man from clay or mud, and when they pronounce the miraculous name of God over him, he must come to life. He cannot speak. They call him golem and use him as a servant. On his forehead is written *'emeth* (truth); every day he gains weight and becomes somewhat larger and stronger than all the others in the house. For fear of him they therefore erase the first letter, so that nothing remains but *meth* (he is dead), whereupon he collapses and turns to clay again (Quoted in G. B. Scholem: *On the Kabbalah and Its Symbolism*).

4.   The truth: what is *oblique*. A monk once asked Kao Tsu: "What is the unique and final word of truth?" . . . The master replied: *"Yes."* I take this answer not as a vague prejudice in favor of general acquiescence as the philosophical secret of truth. I understand that the master, bizarrely opposing an adverb to a pronoun, *yes* to *what*, replies *obliquely;* he makes a deaf man's answer, of the same kind as he made to another monk who asked him: "All things are said to be reducible to the One; but to what is the One reducible?" And Kao Tsu replied: "When I was in the Ching district, I had a robe made for myself which weighed seven *kin*."

Zen

Sobria Ebrietas

vouloir-saisir / will-to-possess

Realizing that the difficulties of the amorous
relationship originate in his ceaseless desire to
appropriate the loved being in one way or another,
the subject decides to abandon henceforth all
"will-to-possess" in his regard.

1.   The lover's constant thought: *the other owes me
what I need*. Yet, for the first time, I am really afraid. I
fling myself on my bed, I mull over the situation and I
decide: from now on, I will not make any attempt to
possess the other.

The N.W.P. (the *non-will-to-possess,* an expression
imitated from the Orient) is a reversed substitute for suicide. Not to kill oneself (for love) means: to take this
decision, not to possess the other. It is the same moment
when Werther kills himself and when he could have renounced possessing Charlotte: it is either that or death
(hence, a Solemn moment).

Wagner

Werther

2.   The *will-to-possess* must cease—but also the *non-
will-to-possess* must not be seen: no oblation. I do not
want to replace the intense throes of passion by "an impoverished life, the will-to-die, the great lassitude."

The N.W.P. is not on the side of kindness, the N.W.P. is
intense, dry: on one hand, I do not oppose myself to the
sensorial world, I let desire circulate within me; on the

Nietzsche

WAGNER: "The world owes me what I need. I must have beauty, brilliance, light." etc. (Quoted in a program of the *Ring* at Bayreuth).

Tao

other hand, I prop it up against "my truth": my truth is to love absolutely: otherwise, I withdraw, I scatter myself, like an army which abandons a siege.

3.   And if the N.W.P. were a tactical notion (at last!)? If I still (though secretly) wanted to conquer the other by feigning to renounce him? If I withdrew *in order* to possess him more certainly? The reversi (that game in which the winner takes the fewest tricks) rests on a feint familiar to the sages ("My strength is in my weakness"). This notion is a ruse, because it takes up a position within the very heart of passion, whose obsessions and anxieties it leaves intact.

Rilke

A final snare: renouncing any will-to-possess, I exalt and enchant myself by the "good image" I shall present of myself. I do not get out of the system: "Armance, exalted . . . by a certain enthusiasm of virtue which was still a way of loving Octave . . .").

Stendhal

4.   For the notion of N.W.P. to be able to break with the system of the Image-repertoire, I must manage (by the determination of what obscure exhaustion?) to let myself drop somewhere outside of language, into the inert, and in a sense, quite simply, *to sit down* ("As I sit calmly, without doing anything, spring comes and the grass grows of its own accord"). And again the Orient: not to try to

Zen

TAO: "He does not show himself and shines. He does not affirm himself and prevails. His work done, he does not attach himself to it, and since he does not attach himself to it, his work will remain" (*Tao Te Ching*).
RILKE: *"Weil ich niemals dich anhielt, halt ich dich fest"* (Because I never hold you, I hold you fast): verses of two songs by Webern, 1911–1912.
STENDHAL, *Armance*.

possess the non-will-to-possess; to let come (from the other) what comes, to let pass (from the other) what goes; to possess nothing, to repel nothing: to receive, not to keep, to produce without appropriating, etc. Or again: "The perfect Tao offers no difficulty, except that it avoids choosing."

Tao

5.   So desire still irrigates the Non-will-to-possess by this perilous movement: *I love you* is in my head, but I imprison it behind my lips. I do not divulge. I say silently to who is no longer or is not yet the other: *I keep myself from loving you.*

Nietzschean accent: "Not to pray any longer—to bless!" Mystical accent: The best and most delectable wine, and also the most intoxicating . . . by which, without drinking it, the annihilated soul is intoxicated, a soul at once free and intoxicated! forgetting, forgotten, intoxicated by what it does not drink and will never drink!"

Ruysbroeck

WRITING

A User Manual

A PRACTICAL GUIDE
TO THE CRAFT OF PLANNING,
STARTING AND FINISHING A NOVEL

David Hewson

BLOOMSBURY PUBLISHING PLC

1 3 5 7 9 10 8 6 4 2

First published in 2012

Bloomsbury Publishing Plc
50 Bedford Square
London WC1B 3DP
www.bloomsbury.com

Copyright © David Hewson 2012

Foreword © Lee Child 2012

David Hewson has asserted his rights
under the Copyright, Designs and Patents Act, 1988,
to be identified as the author of this work

A CIP catalogue record for this book is available
from the British Library

PB ISBN: 978 1 408 15742 8
EPUB ISBN: 978 1 408 15741 1

Available in the USA from Bloomsbury Academic & Professional,
175 Fifth Avenue/3rd Floor, New York, NY 10010.
www.BloomsburyAcademicUSA.com

Typeset by Country Setting, Kingsdown, Kent CT14 8ES
Printed and bound by CPI Group (UK) Ltd, Croydon CR0 4YY